MENDING PIECE BY PIECE AFTER A SUICIDE LOSS

Guided Grief Workbook & Journal to Heal the Survivor's Heart

LINDA FALASCO, LCSW, LICSW

To Rob.
You are my rock.

In Loving Memory of my brother,
Jeffrey Keenan

Contents

Part 1: Understanding Suicide, Loss, & Grief

Part 2: Learning to Live with Grief

Preface

July 18th, 1994. The day my life changed forever. I did not know it then, but from that day forward, I would never be the same again. I was midway through my graduate school program, where I was studying to become a mental health therapist, when I lost my middle brother, Jeffrey, to suicide.

Ever since that day, I have been on an incredibly long and difficult journey of grieving and healing. Amongst the many things that I have come to understand along the way is the fact that it is simply not possible to get over or move past the loss of a loved one. Although I have learned how to cope with the death of my brother, I will never reach a point where I suddenly feel that I have gotten over his passing. The grieving journey is a lifelong one–and it is one that I am still on to this day.

One of the many areas of my life that my brother's passing impacted was my career path. In the wake of his death, I was questioning whether I should finish my graduate school program. I thought that because I had not been able to recognize that my own brother was struggling and needed help, I could not possibly help other people who were dealing with mental health issues. Thankfully, however, with the support and encouragement of my then-boyfriend (now-husband) and some of my professors, I graduated from the program ten months later and became a licensed social worker.

After graduation, I got involved with a number of suicide awareness and prevention organizations as a way to help me process my grief. I became a certified bereavement counselor and received extensive training in grief work. I also began running grief therapy groups and started counseling individuals and families who were grieving.

It was around this time I began to notice that as someone who had lost a sibling, I frequently was lost in the shuffle of things and forgotten by the people around me. Even to this day, I still feel like this sometimes. People often ask me, "How is the family doing?" or, "How is your mom feeling?" but rarely do they ask, "How are you doing, Lindy?" Oftentimes, I have felt like my grief has been disregarded by others and seen as less important than that of people like my parents. In fact, I was expected to take care of my parents as they grieved the loss of their son—but what about me? What about the grief I was experiencing from losing my brother? Unfortunately, even when I have expressed to others that I, too, am grieving and need help, I sometimes have been met with questions like, "Shouldn't you be over this by now?"

Feeling as if I had been completely forgotten by the people in my life following my brother's passing, I began searching for a book or journal that could help guide me through the grieving process. I was not looking for something too intense. I could not handle that at the time. I just wanted something that could help me sort through and understand my loss and the impact it was having on me. Something that would provide me an outlet to express the convoluted jumble of thoughts, feelings, and experiences I was having via creative mediums like writing, drawing, coloring, and collage-making. Something that I could use to both document my grief journey and remember the life of my brother.

I searched for months on end for a grief guide like this but never found something that adequately met all of my grieving needs. As a result, I decided to take things into my own hands by creating a resource for grieving people like me–and that is how this journal came to be.

That being said, the road to putting this journal together was not a short or easy one. I actually began outlining it 15 years ago but had to put it on hold soon after starting it because life just got a bit too crazy; between raising a family, working full-time as a therapist, and processing my own grief, I just did not have enough time or energy to finish it.

During this period, I also experienced multiple losses within my family, which only added to the surplus of things I already had on my plate. Specifically, nearly 20 years after the passing of my brother Jeffrey, tragedy struck again when I lost my youngest brother, Michael, to a drug overdose. As the oldest of three children, Michael's death officially made me the last sibling left in the family. I felt as if I had been left behind by my brothers. I was lost and alone. The grief did not end there, unfortunately. Soon after Michael's passing, I lost my father, nephew, and grandmother within six months of each other. With every additional loss, my grief grew more complicated. The losses became interlaced with one another, each new loss igniting painful feelings from an old one. I was, once again, in desperate need of a resource that would help me process my grief from both my past and present losses.

So in 2022, after an incredibly long detour, I finally got back on the road that I had set out on long ago to create this journal and was able to finish it in the same year. Looking back on what my life was like 15 years ago, I can say with certainty that it was not the right time for me to complete this journal. As a Christian myself, I believe that God's timing is always perfect–and that certainly was the case for this project. Throughout this journal, I share different scripture passages that helped me and others I know through our own grieving journeys. Nonetheless, my hope and prayer is that regardless of your religious alignment or spiritual beliefs, this journal will give you guidance, comfort, and hope as you grieve.

My Message of Hope to You

While reading an online article one afternoon, I came across the following quote by renowned psychiatrist Carl Jung: "I am not what happened to me, I am what I choose to become." I found myself particularly drawn to these words because of their significance in the context of loss and grief.

28 years ago, in the wake of my brother Jeffrey's death, I was faced with a choice: I could either let the grief of losing my brother completely consume me, or I could channel that grief into something positive. Thankfully, I chose the latter.

Whether or not you realize it, you, too, have a choice right now. You can either choose to let your grief overwhelm you to the point that you feel like you are just sort of existing, or you can choose to take back control of your own life; you can choose not only to survive but to thrive again in spite of your loss.

That being said, I know you might not feel like you have the ability to make that kind of choice right now. You may believe that you are permanently trapped in this foggy in-between state of existence, doomed to feel the all-consuming pain of grief for the rest of your life–but that is not true. You just need to learn *how* to start really living again.

In order to truly live your life in the present moment, you must allow yourself to grieve and feel the many emotions that come with it while also learning how to adjust to the world without your loved one in it. Now, I know what you are thinking: "That's impossible! How could I ever get used to living without my loved one?" Trust me, I get it. I was once in your shoes. I understand. So to answer your question: yes, it really is possible to live life in absence of the deceased! I know so, because I have both experienced it myself and witnessed it in the hundreds of other people that I have helped throughout the years.

Healing from your loss and adjusting to this new way of life does not mean forgetting your loved one. Rather, it means figuring out how to keep the feelings of guilt, sadness, and anxiety that have come as a result of your loss from getting in the way of you experiencing the good parts of life. Now, it is okay to stay stuck in the past for a little while. That is a normal part of the grieving process. Remaining engrossed in the past for too long, however, can be detrimental to your quality of life in the present moment. The act of grieving is like holding the past in one hand and the present in the other: the trick is to learn how to balance the two so that you do not let the present moment slip right by you. When you figure out how to do this, you will be able to start living your life again, just as your loved one would have wanted you to do.

After you lose a loved one, you are a different person than who you once were. Like a broken pot, you are cracked in a number of places. You may even be missing a few pieces. Consequently, you may not function in the same way that you used to. When emotions run high, you may start to leak a bit. But like a broken pot, you can be put back together. Slowly, your broken pieces can be replaced and your cracks can be mended. All you need is some (well, maybe a lot of) glue.

So what is the glue? What can you use to piece yourself back together? It can be a lot of things, actually. Your glue may consist of a grief support group, individual counseling, support from family, God, prayer, the Bible, or volunteer work in your community. Everyone's glue is a bit different, just like their grief. As you begin to find the things that work for you, you will be able to start piecing yourself back together and, in doing so, begin living your life once again.

Personally, my glue consists of two things, one being my desire to find a purpose in my loss. After the passing of my brother Jeffrey, I read a book by Iris Bolton titled *My Son... My Son...,* in which Bolton tells the story of how she was able to grieve and heal following the loss of her son to suicide. In one particular chapter, Bolton details an encounter she had with her priest soon after the death of her son, during which he told her that she would find a gift in her son's passing. After reading this, I decided that I, too, wanted to find a gift in the loss of my brother. It was at that moment that I made a conscious choice to take back control of my life by finding a purpose in my pain. What I found was that the loss had given me the gift of compassion and empathy for people in pain, which I could use to help others through their own grief journeys. Since then, I have put this gift into action in a number of ways, from providing individual therapy sessions, to running support groups, to speaking to people around the country about suicide and suicide loss, to hosting an annual candlelight vigil for those who have lost loved ones to suicide.

The second thing that my glue consists of is my Christian faith. In the immediate aftermath of Jeffrey's death, I felt as if I had been forgotten by everyone around me. I believed that I had no one in my life who I could turn to for help, no one who I could truly trust. With seemingly nowhere else to go, I ran to God and found solace in Him. My faith in Him and His everlasting love has given me so much hope; hope that I would be okay, hope that I could trust again, hope that I would one day get to see Jeffrey in Heaven. And it was in this hope that I found the necessary strength to get through the pain and grief I felt, minute by minute, hour by hour, day by day. God has walked by my side through every single step of my grieving journey. At times, he has even carried me. In doing so, He has shown me that it really is possible to find peace and to heal after losing a loved one. As a reminder of His steadfast love for me (and for all of us), I had a bracelet engraved with the phrase "Faith, Hope, Strength, and Love." I wear it nearly every day.

Right now, I know you may feel broken, like you will never be whole again. But I am here to tell you that you will not be broken forever. You can be made whole again. Piece by piece, you can glue yourself back together. Slowly but surely, you can begin to live your life in the present moment again. In order to do so, though, you must first make the conscious choice to begin your journey to healing.

So I ask you this: where are you at right now in your grieving journey, and where will you choose to go? Are you allowing the loss of your loved one to define who you are and how you live, or are you learning how to survive and prosper? Do you feel like you are just existing, or are you truly living? Will you choose to stay stuck in the past forever or will you choose to live life in the present moment?

As someone who was faced with this choice myself, I sincerely hope that you choose to live in the present moment. I hope that you choose to shed the guilt and anxiety that you have carried with you after your loss, even if it is just for a moment. Even in the midst of pain, it is possible to find bits of joy–you just need to look for them. Watch a sunset, listen to your favorite song, spend some time with a furry friend, or share a laugh with your family. Just be in the present.

In doing so, you will not be forgetting or dishonoring your loved one. Grief and joy are not mutually exclusive. You can continue to grieve while also enjoying the pleasant moments that life has to offer. I know that if my brother could, he would say to me, "Lindy, go live your life. I know you love and miss me, but I need you to enjoy what is right there in front of you." And I know that if your loved one could, they would tell you the same exact thing. They would want you to be happy.

So I encourage you to choose life. Choose joy. Choose to embrace the present moment, because that is exactly what your loved one would want for you.

Love,
Lindy

Welcome to Your Journal

You are here because you lost someone very dear to you to suicide. Having lost my own brother to suicide, I understand just how difficult this new journey that you have embarked on is and how excruciatingly painful it can be at times. I am deeply sorry for your loss but am so glad that you found this journal to help you along the way.

Suicide grief is a grief like no other and is something that only another survivor can fully comprehend. Unfortunately, it is one of the most painful experiences a human being can go through. It differs from other forms of grief in ways that make the grieving process especially difficult for the loved ones who are left behind. It affects every aspect of a survivor's life right down to their core beliefs, which may be called into question following their loss. Survivors may lose trust in the people in their lives and in the world around them. They may feel lost and confused, unable to wrap their heads around what the purpose of such a devastating event could be.

At times, you may feel like you are all alone on this grieving journey, like no one understands what you are going through. But I am here to tell you that is not the case. There are many other survivors out there who are grieving too–their grief might just look a bit different than yours (but we will get more into that later). In fact, the Centers for Disease Control and Prevention (CDC) estimates that between 6-32 people are left behind to grieve each individual suicide. In the US alone, approximately 275,000 people become survivors of suicide each year. Just like you, these 275,000 people are left behind to make sense of such an inconceivable loss while the world keeps on spinning around them.

Although grief looks different from person to person, us survivors of suicide are woven together by the common thread that is our suicide loss. So, while we may come from an assortment of backgrounds, hold a variety of spiritual beliefs, and be in a range of different places on our own grief journeys, we are united by this throughline. As you make your way through this journal, then, my hope is that you will realize that you are not alone in your grief and that there are many other survivors out there who are on the same journey as you.

Generally speaking, grief is something that everyone will experience at some point in their life. That said, grief itself is still frequently misunderstood, especially when it is related to suicide loss. In our society, people tend to purposefully avoid experiencing and expressing the kinds of emotions that come with grief, oftentimes putting on a facade so that no one else can see what they are really feeling. Even just talking about grief is taboo to many. Sadly, this is amplified in the context of suicide loss because of the numerous misconceptions and stigmas that surround suicide, keeping many survivors from getting the support they need to properly heal. You may be in a similar situation at this very moment, not having an outlet to sort through the many confusing and painful thoughts and emotions you are having. Hopefully, however, this journal can provide you the space to do just that.

Research has shown that writing can be a highly beneficial tool for people who are grieving. Writing is a creative process that encourages deep self-reflection. This kind of internal exploration of one's thoughts, feelings, and experiences can lead to a deeper understanding and awareness of oneself, as well as the discovery of new ideas, beliefs, and emotions. In this way, writing provides a structured, safe, and healthy way for grieving people to put the various thoughts and feelings they are experiencing as a result of their loss into words and, subsequently, to process them.

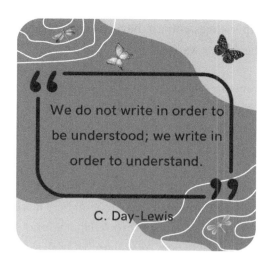

We do not write in order to be understood; we write in order to understand.

C. Day-Lewis

Thus, I created this journal with the intention of providing a safe space for survivors to honestly and openly reflect on their grief journeys. It is meant to be a place where you can come to document the many ups and downs of your grief, and where you can remember the life of your loved one, all without the fear of being misunderstood or judged by others. By giving yourself the opportunity to reflect on your thoughts, feelings, and experiences in this way, you are allowing yourself to begin the process of healing.

This journal is divided into two parts. Part I primarily focuses on teaching you about the concepts of suicide loss and grief, as well as the many ways that they can manifest in your life. It also touches on the importance of engaging in intentional and consistent self-care during periods of grief. In this first part, you will find checklists, questions, and other resources intended to help you both to gain insight into the ways in which your own suicide loss and grief are affecting you and to identify self-care tools that will aid you as you grieve.

Part II is intended to be a place for you to tell your own unique story of loss, grief, and healing. It mainly consists of journal prompts and exercises that will allow you to reflect on your grief journey thus far, share memories of your loved one, and work through your grief in real time. All of these activities are specifically designed to help you better understand the thoughts, emotions, and experiences you are having as you grieve, which, in turn, will set you on the path toward healing.

Now, if you are someone who does not enjoy writing, do not let my repeated use of the word "journal" scare you away! You can respond to the prompts using any creative means you like, whether that be drawing, pasting pictures, or creating a magazine collage. Do what feels right and works best for you.

Another important thing to note is that you do not need to read this journal in chronological order, nor do you have to complete it within a particular time frame. Rather, you should read through it at your own pace and use it in whatever way feels right to you. As you probably already know, every day looks different when you are grieving. Consequently, there may be some days when you need guided exercises to help you express the thoughts and emotions you are experiencing, while on other other days, you may need something more open-ended, like a free-writing activity. There also may be days when you just need a break from it all. That is why I included some coloring pages at the very end of this journal for you to use whenever you need to take your mind off of your grief for a bit. Nonetheless, before you really dive into the journal, I encourage you to familiarize yourself with its contents by simply glancing through the pages.

Throughout the journaling process, please remember to be kind to yourself. The work you will be doing will not be easy by any means, so please allow yourself to show up authentically, no matter what that may look like. If it will be beneficial to you, find a quiet and private place to journal. Try not to filter yourself as you write (or draw, or collage). Give yourself permission to truly feel and express the things that you have been trying your hardest to avoid. Just allow your thoughts and feelings to show up as they are, letting whatever emotions, ideas, and images that may surface come without judgment.

If you find yourself unable to consistently sit down to do the work in this journal, struggling to stick with it when you begin to feel overwhelmed, or just generally feeling unsure of when you should use it, here is a tip that I have suggested to many of my own clients: set aside time specifically dedicated to doing grief work. You can think of it as making an appointment with your grief. So just like you would for a medical check-up or a work meeting, you should reserve a block of time in your day (I suggest 20-30 minutes) to tap into your grief. Do this several times a week if possible, setting a timer before you begin each session. It is important that you have something planned immediately afterward so that when the timer goes off, you will put the journal away until your next grief appointment. This helps with having a sense of control over your grief.

Grief work can be challenging and overwhelming. You may reach a point in your grief journey where you realize that you need additional help from a therapist or counselor. Mental health professionals like this are great at helping people in your shoes develop coping skills to better manage their grief. This is particularly important if you are experiencing impairments in functioning, intense anxiety, panic attacks, or depression. If the death of your loved one was sudden and/or traumatic, you may benefit from seeing a counselor or therapist who specializes in traumatic loss.

Please note that while this book can be used as an additional support to therapy or treatment, it should not be used as a replacement for professional mental health services.

PART I

Understanding Suicide. Loss. & Grief

For everything, there is a season.
and a time for every matter under heaven.
a time to be born. and a time to die.
a time to plant. and a time to pluck up what is
planted. a time to kill. and a time to heal.
a time to break down. and a time to build up.
a time to weep. and a time to laugh.
a time to mourn. and a time to dance.

.Ecclesiastes 3:1-4

Loss & Grief Basics

Generally speaking, the term *loss* refers to the disappearance of something cherished, such as a person, a piece of property, or a way of life. Unfortunately, loss is a frequent and unavoidable part of the human experience. It follows, then, that *grief*–which refers to the emotional response that people have to a loss of any kind–is unavoidable, as well. As the CDC explains, "Grief can happen in response to loss of life, as well as to drastic changes to daily routines and ways of life that usually bring us comfort and a feeling of stability." While grief is natural, it is also a uniquely personal process that varies from individual to individual.

Of the many losses that we inevitably will endure in our lifetime, death is by far the most intense. After the death of a loved one, in particular, it is normal to feel profound grief. In fact, you may be experiencing that at this very moment. You may feel as if your grief is impossible to overcome, like it will completely crush and consume you. But I am here to tell you that is not the case. It is possible to overcome your grief; you just have to work through it. You cannot go under it, over it, or around it. The only way is through.

Grief is Not:
- Time-limited
- One emotion
- One-size-fits-all
- A step-by-step process
- A sign of weakness

In order to understand what grief really entails, it may be helpful to know about the linguistic origins of the word itself.

More than 800 years ago, the Middle English word *gref*–which would eventually evolve into the term *grief* that we use today–was first recorded. It was used to describe "hardship, suffering, pain, [and] bodily affliction."

Gref originates from the old French adjective *grief* (spelled the same as the modern English word), which denotes "wrong, grievance, injustice, misfortune, [and] calamity." This word comes from the old French verb *grever*, meaning to "afflict, burden, [and] oppress."

Going even further back, the old French word *grever* finds its origins in the Latin verb *gravare*, meaning to "make heavy" and "cause grief." *Gravare* comes from the Latin adjective *gravis*, which means "weighty" (and is also where we get the modern English words *grave* and *gravity* from).

Throughout my grieving journey, I have felt many of the things that these root words describe. At times, I have felt like the deaths of my loved ones were *unjust*, like both they and I had been wronged in some way. I have felt like I was lugging around an incredibly heavy *weight* that I just could not get rid of no matter how hard I tried. I have felt like both my mind and my body were *suffering* from the unspeakable *pain* that I was experiencing.

What words would you use to describe your grief? Write them in the space provided below. You can use the words denoted by *grief*'s root words that we talked about above, or you can come up with your own.

_____

_____

_____

_____

_____

_____

_____

GRIEF TIP

Gaining a solid understanding of the concepts of loss and grief will make navigating your grief journey much easier. Knowledge is power, so just knowing key facts about loss and grief can help you take control of your own grief, rather than letting it control you. Below are several truths about loss and grief that, if accepted, will help you develop the endurance and perseverance you need to brave your grief journey.

1. The very worst kind of grief is your own grief
2. The only way out of grief is through it
3. Grief is extremely hard work
4. Grief work is not done alone

Clarifying Some More Terms: *Grief, Mourning, & Bereavement*

After the death of your loved one, you may have started to notice that the words *grief* and *mourning* are often used interchangeably. The two terms, however, actually describe distinct processes that take place in the aftermath of a loss.

On the one hand, *grief* refers to the internal experience that one will go through following a loss. It is an incredibly personal process that differs from individual to individual. This means that there is a wide range of emotions, thoughts, physical sensations, and other reactions that may come as the result of a loss, all of which are a natural part of this internal grieving process.

Mourning, on the other hand, refers to the external experience that one will have after a loss. In other words, it is the way in which people outwardly express the grief that they are feeling internally to the rest of the world. Funerals, religious ceremonies, and the wearing of special clothing are just a few acts of mourning that you may be familiar with. That said, talking about your loss with others, journaling about your grieving experience, or allowing yourself to cry are also ways that you can mourn your loss. This external process of mourning is just as important as the internal process of grieving in your journey toward healing. As psychologist and grief expert Dr. Alan Wolfelt states, "Making the choice to not just grieve but authentically mourn provides you with the courage and confidence to integrate the death of someone loved into your life."

The period of time during which both the internal process of grief and the external process of mourning takes place is known as *bereavement*. This word comes from the adjective *bereaved*, which is used to describe someone who is "suffering the death of a loved one." Just as the processes of grief and mourning are unique to the individual experiencing them, the bereavement period varies vastly from person to person. There are no set rules for how and when bereavement should take place, because no two people will respond in the exact same way to the loss of a loved one.

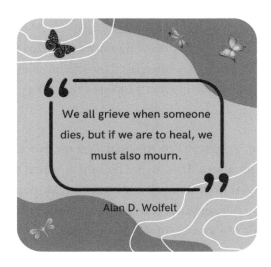

We all grieve when someone dies, but if we are to heal, we must also mourn.

Alan D. Wolfelt

Grieving Styles

As I mentioned in the previous section, the nature of grief is incredibly personal and individualized. It follows, then, that there is not just one correct method of grieving that you must adhere to. There is no singular train of thought that you must follow, no one set of emotions that you must feel (or not feel), and no particular way you must behave in order to grieve the loss of your loved one.

Nonetheless, researchers have found that grieving people exhibit certain emotional, physiological, cognitive, and behavioral patterns, suggesting that there are, in fact, some commonalities in the ways that people grieve. In their book *Men Don't Cry Women Do: Transcending Gender Stereotypes of Grief*, grief experts Terry Martin and Kenneth Doka coined the term *grieving styles* to describe the broad groups that grieving people fall into. Specifically, Martin and Doka identified three particular grieving styles: the intuitive style, the instrumental style, and the blended style (i.e., having both intuitive and instrumental characteristics). The chart below identifies the styles of grieving as identified by Doka and Martin.

Styles of Grieving	
Intuitive Grieving Style	**Instrumental Grieving Style**
• Feels grief intensely • Openly expresses feelings of grief • Expresses sorrow through tears • Allows time to experience inner pain • Is more emotional • Is stereotyped as "female grief"	• Feels grief but less intensely and more physically than intuitive grieving style • Thinks more and feels less • Chooses active ways to express grief • Is reluctant to express feelings • Expresses feelings in private • Is stereotyped as "male grief"

Blended Grieving Style

- Is somewhere in the middle of intuitive and instrumental; uses a little of both styles of grief
- A great majority of grievers fall into this category of grieving
---

As you grieve the loss of your loved one, you may find yourself looking at the people around you and wondering, "Am I the only one grieving? Am I doing something wrong?" all because they are grieving a little bit differently than you. Acknowledging and learning about these different styles of grieving, however, can help you combat these feelings of isolation by opening your eyes to the various ways that those around you are feeling and expressing their own grief.

Additionally, having knowledge of these different grieving styles will help you gain a better understanding of not only how to approach other people who are grieving (e.g., when to talk to them, when to give them space) but also how you want to be approached by others as you grieve. In the same way that you may find it challenging to discern the specific needs of a grieving person, the people around you may not know how to help you during this time. When you have a good sense of your own grieving style, you can communicate your needs with others and, subsequently, open yourself up to receiving the help that you need.

What style of grief do you have?

_____

_____

_____

_____

In what ways do you express your grief? Provide some specific examples.

_____

_____

_____

_____

What style of grief do your family members and/or close friends have? In the table below, write down each person's name, their style of grief, and how they express it.

Name of Family Member or Friend	Style of Grief	How They Express Their Grief

Name of Family Member or Friend	Style of Grief	How They Express Their Grief

Suicide & Suicide Loss

The Complexity of Suicide Loss

The bereavement process for a suicide loss is substantially different than that of a loss brought on by a more normative cause of death, as it is the most severe type of traumatic loss a person can experience. Suicide grief is complex, layered, and generally lasts longer than the grief that follows other kinds of losses.

While many of the thoughts and emotions that a survivor may experience following the suicide of a loved one are similar to those experienced after other types of losses, survivors tend to feel them more intensely. Unlike some other causes of death, suicide is preventable, intentional, unexpected, and highly stigmatized. Consequently, suicide loss often leaves survivors feeling incredibly helpless, isolated, and confused.

Let's take a deeper look into how suicide loss differs from other types of losses:

1. Suicide is considered to be a preventable cause of death. This often leads survivors to experience greater levels of guilt and blame, as well as a heightened sense of rejection and responsibility for the death. As a result, they may start to entertain internally-directed thoughts like "*I should have done more*" or "*I didn't say I love you enough.*" These thoughts and feelings driven by guilt and blame can also be projected onto others, including family members, friends,

doctors, therapists, or the community, as a whole. Sometimes, this externally-directed blame is not warranted. Other times, it may be justified, as the individuals being blamed knew the risk that the deceased individual was at but failed to act. Nonetheless, I highly caution you about falling into the trap of believing the latter, as you may not be able to see the entire picture.

Have you ever felt guilty, or blamed yourself, for the loss of your loved one? If you have, what are some of the guilt- and blame-driven thoughts you have had?

_____

_____

_____

_____

Have you ever blamed someone else for your loss? If you have, who was it? Why did you feel that way?

_____

_____

_____

_____

_____

_____

_____

2. The intentional nature of suicide may lead people to believe that the deceased made the choice to leave them, leaving survivors with a strong sense of abandonment, rejection, and betrayal that is unique to suicide loss. These feelings, in turn, may cause survivors to develop anger toward their loved one, wondering how they could possibly choose to do something like this to them. In her book *Suicide: Why?*, suicidologist Adina Wrobleski says, "Choice implies that a suicidal person can reasonably look at alternatives and select among them. If they could rationally choose, it would not be suicide. Suicide happens when no other choices can be seen." This popular misconception around people's decision to die by suicide is often held by both the surviving loved ones and the community, at large. Unfortunately, it is one of the things that keeps many survivors from accessing the support and resources they need to heal.

Have you ever felt like your deceased loved one abandoned or betrayed you? Have you ever felt angry with them?

_____

_____

_____

_____

_____

_____

_____

_____

Reflecting on the above mentioned quote from Adina Wrobleski about choice in suicide, have you ever found yourself wondering if your loved one made the rational choice to die? If so, do you believe that they did? _

_____

_____

_____

_____

_____

_____

_____

3. While grieving a suicide loss, many people feel isolated, rejected, and abandoned by their family and friends. Support systems that they once had may fall away suddenly due to the highly stigmatized and misunderstood nature of suicide. Sometimes, people avoid individuals who have lost a loved one to suicide simply because they do not know what to say to them or they are afraid that they may upset the person more addressing their loss. Avoiding or ignoring someone who is grieving a suicide loss, however, only leaves them feeling more alone, rejected, and lost.

    I can clearly remember my first experience with this just a few months following my brother Jeff's death. After work one day, I was exiting the train when I saw a "friend" (I put this word in quotes because it was not until after this loss that I learned what a real friend was) walking toward me. I started to smile and make eye contact with her only to be met with a quick glance followed immediately by a look of panic and uneasiness. She then quickly turned around and walked away from me. After this encounter, I was overcome with shame, because I realized I would now be seen and treated in a different way by the people around me.

Following the death of your loved one, have you noticed certain people in your life avoiding you? If so, can you think of a specific instance when this happened? How did you feel at that moment? How did you handle the situation?

_____

_____

_____

_____

_____

4. The unexpected nature of most suicides often leads survivors to seek out an explanation for the death of their loved one. In the immediate aftermath, many survivors feel like their loved one's passing came out of nowhere. Desperately trying to make sense of this abrupt loss, they frequently are haunted by the question "*Why did my loved one take their life?*" Additionally, the sudden nature of suicide leaves many survivors blindsided and shocked, causing them to develop a lingering sense of anxiety, fear, and vulnerability. No matter if the deceased struggled with mental health issues or made previous threats or attempts to end their life, death by suicide is unimaginable and impossible to be prepared for.

How did the sudden death of your loved one leave you feeling?

_____

_____

_____

_____

_____

_____

5. Suicide loss, in general, is a taboo topic surrounded by immense shame and stigma. Unfortunately, some deaths by suicide are characterized by an even greater level of shame and stigma because of the particular mode of death. This stigmatization is largely due to the popular misconception that suicide is a choice, which disregards the role that mental illness and other factors play. Survivors are already part of a highly disparaged group that does not fit easily into, and receives less external support than, other types of bereavement groups. This makes it easy for survivors to feel isolated and unwanted. Sadly, many survivors believe that they need to conceal the way their loved one died because of this stigma, which only increases these feelings of isolation and rejection.

Immediately following my brother Jeff's death, I felt this stigma myself. The day after he passed, I went to the local Catholic church where he had done some volunteer work and had developed a friendship with the new young priest. My brother was not Catholic, but I hoped that because of this relationship he had with the priest, the priest would be willing to officiate his funeral mass. The moment I met the priest, I immediately sensed his genuine concern and compassion for my brother, my family, and me. When I asked him if he would officiate Jeff's funeral mass, he said that because he was not in charge, he had to discuss it with the head priest of the parish. So just a few feet away from me behind a thin curtain, the two priests began the discussion that would thrust me into the world of suicide stigma that I now know all too well. "Was that the boy who killed himself?" the head priest audibly asked the other. "We don't do funerals here for people who commit suicide!" Nothing could have prepared me for the shame and embarrassment that I felt in that moment. Little did I know that it was just the beginning of my experience with people being ignorant or outright rude to me because of my brother's death.

Have you ever had an encounter with the stigma that surrounds suicide? If so, what happened? How did you feel at that moment? How did you handle it?

_____

_____

_____

_____

_____

_____

_____

How has the stigma around suicide affected you? How does it make you feel?

_____

_____

_____

_____

_____

_____

_____

_____

6. Survivors often feel like they have been left behind by their loved one who died by suicide, leading many to be overcome with a sense of helplessness and worthlessness. These feelings are only worsened by the unexpected nature of the death, the stigma surrounding it, the shame and isolation the survivors feel, and the guilt of not being able to help their loved one that haunts them.

    I myself felt helpless and worthless after losing Jeff. At the time, I was in graduate school to become a mental health therapist. Following his death, I started to doubt my ability to help others struggling with mental health issues. "*Who do you think you are?*" I thought. "*Who do you think you're fooling? If you couldn't even help your own brother, what makes you think that you can help someone else?*"

Following the death of your loved one, have you ever felt helpless or worthless? If so, what does that look like for you?

_____

_____

_____

_____

_____

_____

Do you ever feel like your loved one left you behind when they passed? If so, what specific thoughts and emotions come up when you are feeling this way?

_____

_____

_____

_____

_____

_____

Chaos in the Life of a Survivor

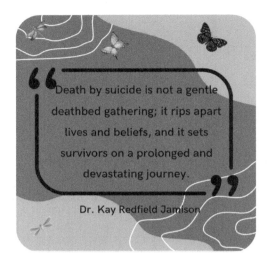

"Death by suicide is not a gentle deathbed gathering; it rips apart lives and beliefs, and it sets survivors on a prolonged and devastating journey."

Dr. Kay Redfield Jamison

Losing someone to suicide is an extraordinarily devastating experience, one that can throw your life into absolute chaos. You may feel like you have been sucked into a tornado of raw, confusing, and painful thoughts and feelings that never seem to stop. Sadness, shock, guilt, rejection, and shame are just a few of the many emotions that survivors have to deal with on a daily basis, oftentimes simultaneously.

Although they may look okay from the outside, many survivors feel like they are going crazy on the inside when they feel and think these kinds of things. Maybe you feel that way, too. I am here to tell you, however, that you are not crazy. This is all just a part of the grieving process. While it might not feel normal, this is the "new normal" that survivors like you have been thrust into involuntarily after losing a loved one to suicide.

Shattered Beliefs

Part of the chaos that comes with suicide loss is the way in which it manages to change so much about you and your life. Its impact is so pervasive that it may go so far as to call into doubt—or even shatter—your core belief system, which dictates how you perceive the world around you. After losing a loved one to suicide, you may begin to question the meaning and purpose of your life. Everything you thought you knew about the world, society, your family, your friends, and yourself is suddenly not so certain anymore. You may find yourself thinking things that never crossed your mind before, like *"My family is not safe,"* *"I can't protect my loved ones,"* or *"I can't trust anything or anyone."* Consequently, you may become overly anxious or develop a sense of skepticism and doubt.

Like the majority of survivors, my core belief system was fractured by my brother Jeff's death. Some of the common thoughts I had (and started to believe) following his passing were:

"If I can't help Jeff, then I can't help anyone else as a therapist."

"Who is going to die next?"

"I think _____ is going to kill themselves because they are upset."

Nonetheless, by seeking help in individual therapy and group therapy, as well as putting in a lot of time and work to heal on my end, I was able to rebuild and repair my belief system—and you can, too!

What core beliefs of yours have been called into doubt or altered following the death of your loved one? Are there things that you now question in your life?

_____

_____

_____

_____

Impact on the Family System

When someone dies by suicide, their death makes a significant and lasting impact on both the individual surviving members of their family and their family unit, as a whole. The suicide of a family member puts an incredible amount of stress on the surviving family, but that does not mean the family system will fall apart. In fact, although some families fracture following this devastating experience, others actually grow closer. The impact that the suicide will have on the family system is determined, in part, by the way in which the family handled conflict and stress prior to the suicide.

It is natural to want to rely on your family for love and support in a difficult time like this. Unfortunately, however, that is not always possible. Even in the best of families, conflict and tension are common following the suicide of one of its members. Changes in communication, dysfunction, marital dissatisfaction, low cohesion, and social isolation are also typical occurrences in family systems dealing with a suicide loss.

That said, families with a higher level of closeness and mutual trust prior to the suicide tend to have more open communication and a greater willingness to share emotions openly with other members. Having healthy coping skills like these is what allows some families to heal from the suicide and grow closer in the process.

For families with little to no previous stress and conflict management skills, however, these issues are often amplified to the point that communication between members and relationships, as a whole, are cut off. When the family system begins to fracture in this way, individual surviving members are left to deal with this traumatic experience on their own.

In addition to the pre-existing stress and conflict management skills that a family has, the role that the deceased individual played in the family also impacts how their death affects the family system and its individual members.

Specifically, if you lost a sibling, you will notice that your parents are completely different people than they were before the suicide. Not only are they grieving the loss of their own child, but they are also grieving the loss of the family they once had. Sadly, people who lose a sibling to suicide often lack a support system because the majority of the external focus and support falls onto the parents. Many sibling survivors report feeling alone, neglected, and left to grieve in silence. As a sibling, you may be expected to put your own needs aside and keep your emotions to yourself so that your parents will not suffer any more than they already have. Unfortunately, this expectation that surviving siblings should suffer in secret can exacerbate the emotional damage they experience. This is why siblings are often called the "forgotten mourners."

From a parent's perspective, losing a child is arguably the most traumatic experience one can have. Parents have an innate sense of responsibility for their child, no matter their age. If their child dies by suicide this sense of responsiblity can become crippling. When a parent loses a child, they are not just grieving the life that was lost but also the dreams they had of a future with their child (and maybe even their grandchildren) that can no longer be. Losing a child to suicide can also adversely impact a parent's ability to care for their surviving children. Feeling overwhelmed by their grief, parents may not be emotionally available enough for their other children, potentially causing disconnects and further isolation amongst family members.

Losing a parent is another incredibly painful experience, one that is only magnified when the death is caused by suicide. Adults and young children alike who lose a parent to suicide often struggle with feelings of aban- donment, guilt, anger, and vulnerability. A deep sense of insecurity may develop in people who lost their parent in such a sudden, unexpected way, leading them to doubt themselves, other people, and the world around them. They may even begin to question their relationship with their de- ceased parent after losing them to suicide, making them wonder what could have been wrong. Survivors who lost a parent also often start to fear that the same thing will happen to them at some point in their life, like they are a ticking time bomb.

When a spouse is lost to suicide, the surviving partner is often left wondering what signs they could have missed that might have prevented this from happening. Some surviving spouses believe that they have failed their partner because they did not fulfill the role of mutual caretaking in their relationship. Others feel abandoned and betrayed by their partners, who so suddenly left them to live without their better half. It can be absolutely devastating to feel like you now have to navigate the world without your righthand person that you may have thought you would spend forever with. That is why when surviving partners grieve, they not only grieve the loss of the person they chose to live their life with, but they also grieve the life they built with their partner and the future they could have had with them.

So regardless of the role that your loved one played in your family system and regardless of the pre-existing communication and stress-management skills your family has, both you and your surviving family have been forever changed by the suicide of your loved one. These changes are not destined to wreak havoc on your family system, but they will make it different. Your loved one's passing has left seats empty, roles vacant, and dreams unfulfilled. Their presence is something that can never be replaced, something that you and your family now must learn to live without.

What role did your loved one play in your family? Were they your sibling, your spouse, your parent, etc.? How has the role that they played affected your family system now that they are gone?

_____

_____

_____

_____

_____

_____

_____

_____

Prior to the death of your loved one, how did your family handle stress and conflict? How has that affected the impact that the suicide has had on you and your family?

_____

_____

_____

_____

_____

_____

_____

In what other ways has your family system changed since the death of your loved one?

_____

_____

The Search for "Why"

After losing a loved one to suicide, survivors tend to spend much of their time trying to wrap their heads around why the death occurred. *"Why did this happen?"* they wonder. *"Why did they do this?"* The need to explore these "why" questions preoccupies all survivors to some degree.

Developing an acceptable narrative for why the suicide occurred is one of the most essential healing tasks for suicide loss survivors. By searching for answers to these "why" questions, survivors are able to regain some sense of control over their grief and life. Doing so can also alleviate survivors' guilt and fear that they were somehow responsible for the suicide of their loved one.

It's important to note that no one else can answer the question *"Why?"* for you. This is something deeply personal that you must search for on your own. I realize that might be an intimidating quest to take on by yourself, especially given how loud and all-consuming these "why" questions can be at times. Eventually, though, you will find an answer that works well enough for you, that satisfies your desire to understand your loved one's passing, that silences the voice in your head that keeps asking, *"Why?"* even for just a little bit. That voice might come back now and again, but it will not be as loud and constant. You may have to restart the search for the answer to these "why" questions from time to time. Some survivors battle with their "*Why?*" for their entire life. Whatever the case may be, it is all normal for this abnormal kind of loss.

Use the space below to write, draw, collage, etc. about your "*Why?*"

_____

_____

_____

_____

_____

_____

_____

_____

_____

_____

_____

_____

_____

The Effects of Suicide Loss

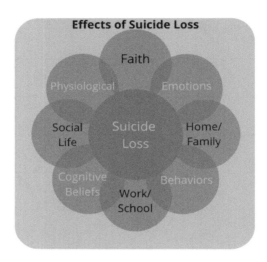

As you likely already have come to realize, the life you are living now is completely different from the life you were living before the death of your loved one. Not only are you experiencing a range of new thoughts and emotions internally, but you are also being faced with a variety of new situations externally.

Although suicide grief looks different for everyone, research has identified a number of specific experiences that survivors tend to go through as they grieve the loss of their loved one. Interestingly, some of these effects are unique to suicide grief, making it a bit different than grief related to other causes of death. Generally speaking, suicide grief is an extraordinarily intense experience that oftentimes is more painful than other forms of grief. What's more is that suicide grief has the ability to permeate nearly every aspect of an individual's life, sometimes without them even realizing it. A loved one's suicide has the ability to impact a survivor physically, emotionally, cognitively, socially, behaviorally, and spiritually, demonstrating just how deep and wide its effects can run.

I know from my own grief journey just how confusing, disconcerting, and scary it is to be confronted with these various grief-related symptoms, especially when you do not realize what is truly causing them. That is why it is so important to learn about the numerous ways grief can impact people and use that knowledge to identify the ways your grief is impacting you. By taking the time to understand and acknowledge how grief affects your body, mind, and soul, you will start to feel more comfortable with, and gain a sense of control over, your grief journey.

So without further ado, let's explore the various ways that suicide loss can impact the life of a survivor like you.

Emotional Symptoms

Following the suicide of your loved one, you may have started to experience a painful, overwhelming, and outright exhausting mixture of emotions.

While potentially worrisome, this bombardment of feelings is completely normal in the suicide grieving process. Shock, worry, guilt, and shame are just a few of the many emotions that survivors may feel as they grieve the loss of their loved one. The intensity, complexity, and unpredictability of these emotions may leave you feeling vulnerable, confused, and alone. Sometimes, you may even feel like you are losing your mind–but I want you to know that you are not. You are simply grieving.

While there is no way to prepare for such an intense storm of emotions as this, learning about the many feelings that can come with suicide grief and identifying the ones that you have felt is a great way to make yourself feel less alone and more in control of your grieving process.

Shock

In the immediate aftermath of a suicide loss, survivors often go into a state of shock and denial. The numbness and disbelief that are commonly felt during this period can last anywhere from a few weeks to a few months after the suicide.

While in this state of shock, you may feel completely detached from both yourself and the world around you. Objects in front of you, for instance, may look dream-like, or they may appear to be farther away than they really are. Your chest or throat may feel tight in a way that makes it difficult to breathe or your stomach may feel upset. You also may feel a general sense of heaviness weighing on you.

Whatever your experience may be, this state of shock is your body and mind's way of protecting you. It is what allows you to carry on minute by minute, day by day, week by week, in spite of the chaos that surrounds you. While it may not seem like it, this state of shock guards you from immediately feeling the full force of the pain and emotions that your sudden loss has caused. In a sense, this state of shock acts as a shield, keeping you safe from the reality of what is happening while you are in such a vulnerable state. This is what allows some survivors to talk with police, funeral home employees, family members, and others in the immediate aftermath of a suicide.

Over time, this state of shock wears off, gradually easing you into the intense storm of grief-driven emotions so that you are not completely immobilized by them. As this shield falls away, then, you will begin to feel the wide spectrum of emotions more deeply.

Additionally, the sudden nature of suicide, which offers no time for farewells or resolutions with loved ones, causes many survivors to fall into a state of disbelief or outright denial immediately following the death. During this time, many survivors convince themselves that the death was an accident. Others believe that their loved one did not actually die and will be back soon from wherever they seem to have wandered off to. While denial, like shock, can act as a protective force, it can also be harmful if taken too far. Specifically, denying the reality of the suicide for too long can keep survivors from experiencing the natural grieving process, which can make the repressed emotions and other reactions feel far more overwhelming down the road.

In the immediate aftermath of your loved one's suicide, did you experience shock? If so, what was that experience like?

_____

_____

_____

_____

_____

Some survivors view the shock they experienced as having been a gift that protected them during a time of vulnerability. How do you view your shock?

_____

_____

_____

_____

_____

_____

Were you ever in a state of disbelief or denial about your loved one's death? If so, what did you tell yourself about what happened?

_____

_____

_____

_____

_____

_____

Guilt

Guilt is an emotion that accompanies all kinds of grief, but it is particularly common and oftentimes compounded for survivors due to the nature of suicide. It is typically after that initial flood of emotions that the guilt begins to set in. Of all the emotions that come with suicide grief, guilt is arguably the most difficult to confront, in part because of the distorted or outright false ideas that it can put in survivors' heads.

Some of the guilty thoughts that my clients have shared with me over the years are:

- *"This is your fault. He only got in trouble because of the things you did."*
- *"You wished he would just get it over with, so this must be your fault."*
- *"You should have known something was wrong."*

Guilt also strikes at times when survivors take their mind off their grief for a moment to laugh or be happy. *"How could you laugh when you just lost your son?"* their mind might say. *"You must not have loved her that much if you are already having fun."*

Moreover, guilt is rooted in feelings of regret and remorse for either something that you believe you did wrong or something you wish you had done. Consequently, guilt is often accompanied by self-blame, which leads many survivors to spend a substantial amount of time racking their brains for things they did or did not say or do that could link them to the suicide.

In an attempt to escape these internally-pointed feelings of guilt and blame, many survivors start blaming others for the suicide of their loved one. Doctors, therapists, and God are common external targets that survivors put their blame on. Arguably the toughest situation is when that blame is put on family members or friends, as it can make seeking comfort and support from those people incredibly challenging, if not impossible. That said, outwardly directing the blame in this way is completely natural and understandable given its ability to grant survivors a sense of relief, even if that relief is temporary.

What are some of the guilty thoughts you are experiencing?

_____

_____

_____

_____

_____

Have you blamed yourself or others for the death of your loved one? If so, why?

_____

_____

_____

_____

_____

_____

Is anyone around you blaming themselves or others for the death? If so, who?

_____

_____

_____

_____

_____

_____

_____

_____

Anger

Anger is another common emotion in suicide grief and is arguably one of the most frightening to experience, especially when it is directed toward the deceased. Even though this kind of anger with the deceased is extremely common amongst survivors, many feel guilty for having that kind of feeling and, as a result, do not outwardly express it.

Survivors may also direct their anger at a range of other people, things, and situations, such as family members, God, or the healthcare system. When I lost my brother Jeff, I would just be walking around or driving and suddenly feel myself getting angry with people and at things that did not actually warrant such a reaction. In hindsight, I realize that I was so often angry with the world around me because it felt like a safer option than delving into the true source of my pain.

Anger can quickly turn into depression, so if you have been experiencing it in the aftermath of your loss, I encourage you to talk about it with someone, whether they be a friend, a family member, or a mental health professional.

Have you experienced anger following the death of your loved one? If so, what or who have you been angry with?

_____

_____

_____

_____

_____

_____

_____

What does your anger look like? Use the space below to write about it, draw what it looks like, etc.

_____

_____

_____

_____

_____

_____

_____

_____

_____

Do you try to avoid anger? If so, why?

_____

_____

_____

_____

_____

_____

_____

How do you express your anger?

_____

_____

_____

_____

_____

_____

_____

God will wipe away every tear from their eyes, and death shall be no more, neither shall there be mourning, nor crying, nor pain anymore, for the former things have passed away.

Revelation 21:4

Depression

Although grief and depression are distinct from one another, some of their symptoms actually overlap. In fact, depression appears to be a common response to suicide deaths. Given the many intense emotions that survivors deal with but oftentimes cannot express to others due to the stigma around suicide, it is no surprise that they are prone to developing depressive symptoms as they grieve.

Generally speaking, depression is characterized by prolonged sadness with an inability to expect happiness or pleasure. Symptoms of depression include sleep problems, listlessness, low energy level, fatigue, decreased interest in sex, overeating or undereating, and feeling sad or low. If you are experiencing depression, you may find it difficult to laugh or have fun.

You may struggle to get yourself out of bed to go to work or school. You may find it challenging to talk to your friends, or you may start isolating yourself from other people altogther.

Do you feel like you are able to share your emotions openly with others? Why or why not?

_____

_____

_____

_____

_____

Have you, or are you, experiencing symptoms of depression? If so, what does your depression look like? Use the space below to write about it, draw what it looks like or collage.

_____

_____

_____

_____

_____

_____

_____

Anxiety

After losing a loved one to suicide, survivors often develop anxiety–but that anxiety can range anywhere from experiencing worry from time to time, to having panic attacks, to feeling a constant and all-consuming sense of dread.

One common experience is the sudden development of new fears. Some examples of fears triggered by suicide loss that my clients have shared with me are the fear of being left alone, the fear of being in the place where their loved one died, the fear of relationships, the fear that other people are going to take their own lives, the fear of the word suicide, and the fear that they themselves are going to want to kill themselves at some point.

Other common symptoms of anxiety that you may be experiencing are trouble concentrating, restlessness, nervousness, ruminating thoughts, issues sleeping, worry about changes in routine, and difficulty separating yourself from loved ones.

Anxiety can manifest itself through physical symptoms, as well. Those symptoms can be so intense to make you believe that something is medically wrong with you when they are, in fact, your body's physiological response to being under prolonged stress. Physical anxiety symptoms include an increased heart rate, rapid breathing, sweating, trembling, feeling weak or tired, and experiencing gastrointestinal problems.

Regardless, if you ever experience any physical symptoms that cause you concern, please consult with a physician to rule out any serious medical issues.

Have you experienced anxiety following the death of your loved one? If so, use the space below to write, draw, collage, etc. about what your anxiety looks like.

_____

_____

_____

_____

_____

_____

_____

_____

_____

_____

Whirlwind of Emotions

It always seems to be that just when the world around you expects you to be over the death of your loved one, your emotions come roaring back like a whirlwind, stronger than ever. In my experience working with survivors, many people are surprised by the intensity of their emotional symptoms after the first year. Many of them have even reported feeling worse after that first year. While it is a shock to hear that, I assure you that it is completely normal for this abnormal grieving process.

As time goes on, though, these sudden whirlwinds of grief-driven emotions will become less intense and a bit more predictable. You will learn how to navigate the sudden onslaughts of painful thoughts and feelings and, subsequently, will be able keep moving forward and living your life.

Exercise:

While everyone's experience with grief is different, there are a number of emotions that survivors of suicide often experience. Below is a list of emotions commonly felt by those left behind by suicide. Take a look at it and check off the emotions that you have experienced following your loss.

- ☐ Shock
- ☐ Disbelief
- ☐ Shame
- ☐ Numbness
- ☐ Denial
- ☐ Confusion
- ☐ Anxiety
- ☐ Panic
- ☐ Worry
- ☐ Fear
- ☐ Anger
- ☐ Sadness
- ☐ Despair
- ☐ Guilt
- ☐ Loneliness
- ☐ Isolation
- ☐ Irritability
- ☐ Rage
- ☐ Yearning
- ☐ Hopelessness
- ☐ Self-Pity
- ☐ Overwhelmed
- ☐ Relief
- ☐ Hurt
- ☐ Powerlessness
- ☐ Helplessness

Physical Symptoms

Although most people are aware of the emotional impact that grief can have, many are unfamiliar with the ways in which it can manifest in the physical body. Grieving individuals frequently report not feeling like themselves after their loss and begin to complain of physical ailments, such as fatigue, heartache, trouble breathing, and digestive issues.

After you experience a loss, grief sends your body into a state of stress. Your bloodstream is suddenly flooded with stress hormones that can affect your entire body, from your heart, to your intestines, to your skin, to your immune system. For example, research has shown that the inflammatory response rises and immune cell function falls in individuals who are grieving. This means that people are more susceptible to getting sick following the loss of a loved one.

These physical symptoms may linger around for far more than a few days or weeks after a loss. Months and years can go by, and you still may feel the physical effects of grief in your body. Nonetheless, over time, many of these symptoms should resolve on their own. It is important to note that if you are experiencing intense physical pain or have any concern about your symptoms, you should consult with a physician to rule out any serious medical conditions.

Trauma lives in the body and stays there for a very long time. Even when the mind forgets the trauma, then, it may resurface in the body. It is not uncommon to experience the same physical symptoms—like a stomach ache or chest pain—that you experienced at the time of your loved one's death months or even years later. This phenomenon is known as a "body memory" and can happen even when you are not actively thinking about your loved one or their death. The reason this happens is because trauma has the ability to change the way your brain and nervous system functions. On top of the "body memories," trauma can lead to dysregulation within your body, causing symptoms like headaches, dizziness, and chest pain.

As a result of the trauma they endured due to their loved one's suicide, survivors may also experience *hypervigilance*, which is the state of being constantly on guard and susceptible to overreaction. If you are in a hypervigilant state, you may notice yourself being intensely aware of your surroundings and continually on high alert looking for threats. This is your body's way of protecting you from the danger that it was alerted to back when your loved one died. What your body does not know, however, is that there is no longer any danger; it is reacting to the past, not the present.

Trauma responses that are stored in the body, such as hypervigilance and "body memories," can prevent survivors from properly healing from their loss. If you are experiencing any of these kinds of symptoms to the extent that they are interfering with your quality of life, I encourage you to seek professional help. Specifically, trauma therapies focusing on regulating and calming the nervous system while integrating traumatic memories may be beneficial to you as you work to heal your body and mind.

I, too, experienced many of these physical symptoms of suicide grief after the death of my brother Jeff. The stomach and body aches, the fatigue, the brain fog, the pain in my heart—all of it remained for a good few years after Jeff passed. I was almost constantly in a state of hypervigilance, to the point where if someone came up behind me and just said my name, I would be sent straight into a state of panic, screaming as if I was being attacked. Even to this day, there are certain times of the year that I will feel overly tired, my body will feel heavy, and my stomach will feel nauseous, regardless of whether I am actively thinking about the death of my brother.

Exercise:

Below is a list of physical symptoms commonly felt by grieving people. Take a look at it and place a check beside the symptoms you have experienced following your loss.

☐ Fatigue
☐ Loss of energy
☐ Digestive problems
☐ Headaches
☐ Body aches
☐ Sore muscles
☐ Muscle weakness
☐ Chest pains
☐ Shortness of breath
☐ Nausea
☐ Vomiting
☐ Stomach pain
☐ Weight loss/gain
☐ Brain fog

☐ Memory loss
☐ Weakened immune system/ frequently sick
☐ Dry mouth
☐ Dehydration
☐ Hair loss
☐ Dizziness
☐ Blood pressure issues
☐ Empty feeling or "knot" in the stomach
☐ Tightness in the chest or throat
☐ Heartache

How is your body responding to your loss?

_____

_____

_____

_____

_____

_____

Cognitive Symptoms

Grief can also affect the way our brain functions. Following a loss, our brain is so busy processing and dealing with the resulting grief that many of its other responsibilities, like concentrating and remembering, fall by the wayside.

As a result, you may feel as though you have what many grieving people describe as "grief fog." You may find it difficult to think clearly, to make decisions, to keep up in conversations, or to remember to do things. Your brain may spin typical thoughts into maladaptive cognitions. You may even struggle to keep up with everyday tasks—like showering, eating, or paying bills—that at one time required no thought or effort.

I know these cognitive symptoms can be incredibly frustrating and over-whelming, but please remember to be patient and gentle with yourself. You are not going crazy or losing your mind or doing anything wrong. You are simply experiencing a natural part of the grieving process.

Exercise:

Take a look at the following list of common cognitive symptoms caused by grief and put a checkmark next to the symptoms you have experienced:

- ☐ Loss of concentration
- ☐ Inability to make decisions
- ☐ Impaired judgment
- ☐ Losing things
- ☐ Forgetfulness
- ☐ Decreased motivation
- ☐ Confusion
- ☐ Difficulty processing information
- ☐ Altered perception of time
- ☐ Preoccupation with thoughts of life or death of loved one
- ☐ Disbelief
- ☐ Hearing the voice of loved one

The way that you feel about yourself and the world around you is largely dictated by your thoughts. Consequently, if you regularly allow yourself to think a certain way, you will begin to believe in, and identify with, those thoughts. Following the loss of a loved one, it is completely normal to have an influx of negative thoughts, such as *"I should have spent more time with them," "I was not a good daughter,"* or *"I should have done more."*

That said, if these negative thoughts develop into a consistent stream of negative thinking, they may begin to wreak havoc on your mental state and overall well being.

Parents of children who died by suicide, for instance, are often haunted by an all-consuming sense of failure and heavy guilt around a perceived mistake they made in raising their child. *"I didn't do enough," "I didn't take care of them,"* or *"I pushed them too much,"* are just a few of the lies parents think to themselves. The case is similar for surviving spouses, who often feel a sense of failure for not fulfilling the role of mutual caretaking they believe they had in their relationship. For both surviving parents and spouses, this feeling of failure can lead to the cognitive belief that they are not good enough, which, in turn, can cause low-self esteem and feelings of worthlessness.

Thus, it is crucial that you learn how to notice and examine the thoughts you are having in real time. For example, is a particular thought negative and damaging or is it positive and constructive? It is also important that you know how to reframe those negative thoughts into more balanced thoughts. While I know it is easier said than done, possessing the ability to determine the quality and validity of your thoughts and then reframe them in a more balanced, healthier way will help you stay in control of your emotions, behaviors, and physical feelings as you continue to grieve and heal.

Exercise:

Below is a list of negative cognitive thoughts that people commonly experience after a loss. Go through the list and highlight, circle, or check off all of the negative thoughts that you have experienced. Then, write a new, more balanced thought next to it. Feel free to use the blank spaces to write additional thoughts that you have had.

Negative Thought	New Thought
I should have done more.	*I did the best I could with what I knew.*
Why didn't I do something to help him?	*I did the best I could with what I knew.* *He knows I loved him and did all I could.*
If only I ...	
I wish I ...	
I am not good enough.	
Why is this happening?	
I am a failure.	
I should have ...	
I would have ...	
I could have...	
What could I have done differently?	
No one understands me.	
Bad things always happen to me.	
What did I miss?	
It's all my fault.	

Negative Thought	New Thought
What did I do to deserve all this?	
I must be a bad person for this to have happened.	
What is happening to me?	
I have no control.	
How can I deal with all this?	
I hurt so bad. Will I ever feel peace?	
Is my loved one in Heaven?	
Will I ever feel happy or joyful again?	
My loved one abandoned me, who else will leave me?	
Where are my friends when I need them?	
I feel so alone.	

Negative Thought	New Thought

Next time you find yourself having any of these negative thoughts, try to use the skills that you practiced in this activity by examining the thoughts and reframing them in a more balanced manner.

Spiritual Manifestations

According to Elizabeth Scott, PhD, spirituality is "the broad concept of a belief in something beyond the self. It may involve religious traditions centered on the belief in a higher power, but it can also involve a holistic belief in an individual connection to others and to the world as a whole." Generally speaking, spirituality is a deeply personal experience that allows people to find meaning in their lives.

While your relationship with spirituality may change over time, death can have a particularly potent impact on it. This is because death forces you to reflect on existential topics that you might not frequently think about, such as the purpose of our time here on earth, the reason that people die, and what comes after death.

Just like grief, spirituality is a unique and personal experience. Consequently, the effect that grief has on spirituality varies from person to person. For some, the death of a loved one may test their spiritual beliefs, causing them to feel angry with the higher power(s) that they believe in. For others, their faith may be the thing that they find solace in after their loss. They may even experience a deepening of their faith as a result.

That said, spirituality, at its very core, is rooted in connection–connection to a higher power, to other people, to the universe–, which can be an immense comfort in the grieving process. Thus, it is important that you try to nurture your own spirituality as you make your way through your own grieving journey. There are a number of different ways that you can do this, from praying, to meditating, to reading scripture, to doing yoga, to going to church, to spending time in nature.

After Jeff's death, I felt like the foundation that I had built my life on had crumbled, like I could not take a step in any direction without getting caught up in the ash and debris that had been left. As I felt myself losing faith in everything around me, however, I was able to put my trust in God– and my faith in Him grew stronger because of it. He took me by the hand and guided me through the rubble into a clearing, making sure that I did not stumble along the way.

Exercise:

Below are some questions to help you explore, and deepen your awareness of, how the loss of your loved one has impacted you spiritually.

How would you describe spirituality? How do you nurture your spirituality?

_____

_____

_____

_____

_____

Has your spirituality been impacted by your loss? If so, how?

_____

_____

_____

_____

_____

Have you been able to find solace in your spiritual beliefs as you grieve your loved one? If so, describe what that has been like.

_____

_____

_____

_____

_____

If not, what has it been like for you?

_____

_____

_____

_____

Social Impact

When you lose a loved one, the grief that follows can impact both how people interact with you and how you interact with others. Unfortunately, the social effects of grief are often magnified when the death is caused by suicide because of how incredibly stigmatized suicide is.

For one, you may find yourself not having the energy or desire to be around other people. The exhaustion, brain fog, and overall negative mental state that you may be in can make the small talk that frequently occurs in social settings seem difficult and even trivial. While your friends sit around and talk about yesterday's football game, for instance, you may find yourself thinking, "*Who cares what the score was? My mom just died.*" It's like the world is going on around you like nothing is wrong and you just want to shout, "Stop! Does no one care that I am grieving?" This decreased desire and ability to socialize with others may cause you to start isolating yourself, whether it is purposeful or not.

Another social challenge you may face as a survivor is your friends and family not acknowledging your grief. Maybe they never bring it up in conversation with you and go on with their lives like nothing has happened. Maybe they stop making an effort to spend time with you. Maybe they even outright ignore you because they do not know what to say. All of this can be incredibly hard to deal with, especially as you try to move through the indescribable pain you are feeling in the wake of your loss. Sometimes, all you want is to talk to someone about your loved one and your grief. To not have your grief acknowledged by those around you, then, may leave you feeling misunderstood and alone.

Even though you are tired, it is important that you let the people in your life know what you need. Remember that they are not mind readers. It may surprise you, but most people actually want to help you as you go through this grieving process–they just may not know how to go about doing so. The best thing for you to do, then, is to tell them exactly how they can help you. For instance, if you want to talk about your loved one and your loss, you should bring those topics up yourself, as other people may be afraid to do so first. They may be scared to ask you how you are or to say your loved one's name because they do not want to upset you. What they do not realize, however, is that talking about your loved one is exactly what you want to do as you continue to process and grieve their death.

All that said, give yourself permission to say no to social activities if they do not feel like the right thing for you to do at that moment. If you are unsure of whether you want to do something and need to wait until the day of, just let others know ahead of time. Remember that it is normal to feel less social while grieving, so allow yourself the time and space that you need to heal.

Exercise:

Below are several questions intended to help you explore, and deepen your awareness of, how your loss has impacted you socially.

How have your social relationships changed after the loss of your loved one?

Do you feel like anyone has pushed you away? Has anyone ignored you or avoided you? If so, who has acted in this way?

_____

_____

_____

_____

How do you feel and react when people act in these ways?

_____

_____

_____

_____

_____

Has your desire and/or ability to socialize with other people changed since you lost your loved one?

_____

_____

_____

_____

_____

Elephant in the Room

by Terry Kettering

There's an elephant in the room.
It is large and squatting,
so it is hard to get around it.

Yet we squeeze by with,
"How are you?" and "I'm fine,"
and a thousand other
forms of trivial chatter.

We talk about the weather;
We talk about work;
We talk about everything else-
except the elephant in the room.

There's an elephant in the room.
We all know it's there.
We are thinking about the elephant
as we talk together.

It is constantly on our minds.
For, you see, it is a very big elephant.
It has hurt us all, but we don't talk about
the elephant in the room.

Oh, please say his/her name.
Oh, please, say "....." again.
Oh, please, let's talk about
the elephant in the room.

For if we talk about his/her death,
Perhaps we can talk about his/her life.
Can I say "....." to you
and not have you look away?
For if I cannot,

then you are leaving me
Alone...in a room...
with an elephant.

Behavioral Responses

Lastly, grief can also impact the way that you behave. Not only do the behavioral effects of grief vary from person to person, but they may also vary for individuals depending on the day. You may start avoiding certain activities or isolating yourself from other people, because you may be fearful of triggering a traumatic memory or of becoming emotional in public. Or you may be filling up your calendar with social events, household chores, work–anything that will help you stay busy and keep you from thinking. Maybe you have started carrying around an object that belonged to your loved one, listening to a voicemail they left you on repeat, or wearing an item of their clothing. Or maybe you just feel like you are walking around in a daze.

For survivors, specifically, it is not uncommon to repeat the same story or to say the same thing about your loved one over and over again. This is a natural part of the healing process that is, unfortunately, often misunderstood by others. Imitating the deceased or adopting their mannerisms are also common behaviors for survivors, especially amongst siblings or children. Parents who lost a child to suicide may refuse to move or change anything in their homes in an attempt to keep things as they were when their child was alive. All of these things are completely normal behaviors for grieving suicide survivors.

Exercise:

Below are several questions intended to help you explore, and deepen your awareness of, how your loss has impacted you behaviorally.

How have your behaviors changed following the loss of your loved one?

_____

_____

_____

_____

_____

_____

_____

_____

_____

Have you experienced any of the following:

- ☐ Trouble falling asleep
- ☐ Trouble staying asleep
- ☐ Sleeping too much
- ☐ Searching and/or calling out for your loved one
- ☐ Overeating
- ☐ Undereating
- ☐ Increased smoking
- ☐ Increased alcohol use
- ☐ Sexual difficulties
- ☐ Socially isolating
- ☐ Not engaging in conversations
- ☐ Visiting places that remind you of your loved one
- ☐ Carrying or treasuring objects of your loved one
- ☐ Assuming mannerisms or traits of your loved one
- ☐ Sighing
- ☐ Crying spells
- ☐ Avoiding reminders of your loved one
- ☐ Retelling the story of your loss
- ☐ Not talking about your loss

While some behaviors can actually be beneficial to you as you grieve, other behaviors can inhibit and even be detrimental to your grieving process. Have you engaged in any behaviors that you realize may not be helpful to you?

_____

_____

_____

_____

_____

_____

On the flipside, is there anything you have been doing that has brought you comfort as you grieve?

_____

_____

_____

_____

_____

_____

Secondary Losses

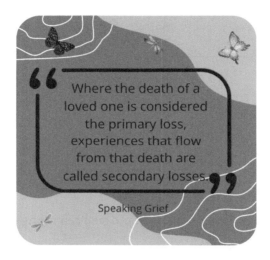

> Where the death of a loved one is considered the primary loss, experiences that flow from that death are called secondary losses.
>
> Speaking Grief

While you may not be aware of it, the loss of your loved one most likely is not the only loss that you are grieving right now. The death of a loved one creates a sort of ripple effect, causing multiple additional losses in the lives of those left behind. These are known as *secondary losses.* Loss of a home, daily routines, future plans, personal identity, and roles that your loved one played in your life are just a few examples of secondary losses that you might experience following the death of your loved one.

Now, don't let the word *secondary* fool you–secondary losses can be just as painful and difficult to process as the death of your loved one. In this way, secondary losses can further complicate the already convoluted and difficult grieving process you are going through.

Although they are a normal part of grief, secondary losses frequently go unrecognized for long periods of time–or forever in some cases. This is due, in part, to the fact that secondary losses are not as public as the loss of a life. Consequently, they often go undetected both by the person who has experienced the loss and by those around them.

Given the tremendous weight that these secondary losses can add to your already heavy grief burden, it is important to take inventory of them and their impact on you.

Exercise:

Take your time to review the following list of secondary losses, checking off the ones that you have experienced in the past or are currently experiencing:

- ☐ Loss of income
- ☐ Loss of relationships
- ☐ Loss of faith
- ☐ Loss of role (e.g., sister, father, mentor)
- ☐ Loss of hopes & dreams
- ☐ Loss of financial stability
- ☐ Loss of companionship
- ☐ Loss of time
- ☐ Loss of home
- ☐ Loss of security
- ☐ Loss of support system
- ☐ Loss of confidence
- ☐ Loss of family unit
- ☐ Loss of truth as you knew it
- ☐ Loss of identity

What other secondary losses are you experiencing?

_____

_____

_____

_____

_____

_____

_____

_____

_____

_____

_____

_____

_____

_____

_____

Exercise: Ripple Effect

The following activity is designed to help you visualize the secondary losses you have experienced and the ways in which they have impacted you. By acknowledging these additional losses and seeing them for what they are, you will allow yourself the opportunity to properly grieve and heal from them.

In the diagram below, start by writing the name of the person you lost in the center bubble. Then, in the neighboring bubbles, write down any secondary losses that have been triggered by the loss of your loved one, as well as the ways in which those secondary losses have affected you. For example, the death of your loved one may have resulted in the loss of your daily running partner, which has left you feeling unmotivated to run and exercise. If you need help thinking of secondary losses, you can refer back to the list in the previous exercise.

The Importance of Self-Care in Grieving

Self care is not selfish. You must fill your own cup before you can fill others.

The term *self-care* refers to the act of taking care of your mind, body, and soul by engaging in activities that reduce stress, promote good health, and increase overall well-being. Generally speaking, our current societal culture encourages people to always be on the go, which makes it difficult to find the time, space, and energy to take care of ourselves in this way. When we grieve, then, self-care can become an incredibly daunting and seemingly impossible task.

As you make your way through the grieving process, you may find yourself becoming easily overwhelmed by even the most simple of tasks. Even the activities that are essential to your health and well-being–like eating, drinking, and moving around–may become too much for you, and you may stop doing them altogether. In an attempt to escape the intense feelings of grief you are experiencing, you may also start doing things that can be harmful to you in both the short and long term. Overeating, rushing into new relationships, or using drugs and alcohol are just a few examples of these self-harming behaviors you might find yourself taking part in.

During a time of such intense pain, you may find it difficult to recognize the habits that you are making and breaking, let alone to find the energy to do what is best for your health and well-being. Nonetheless, it is so important that you try your best to keep up with your self-care as you grieve the loss of your loved one–and if it is just too hard to do so, ask the people in your life whom you really trust to help you. You may be surprised by how many people actually want to help you but simply do not know how to go about doing so. The best way to get the help you need, then, is to tell them exactly how they can help you take care of your health and well-being, whether that be by making you a meal, taking a walk with you, or giving you gentle reminders to shower and get-dressed every day.

Exercise:

Below is a list of good self-care activities that can be done on a regular basis. Read through them and check off the ones that you are currently doing:

- ☐ Feed yourself at least 3 times a day
- ☐ Take a shower
- ☐ Spend time outside
- ☐ Stretch
- ☐ Do yoga
- ☐ Exercise
- ☐ Get a massage
- ☐ Focus on taking deep breaths
- ☐ Try something new

- ☐ Stay hydrated and keep your water bottle filled
- ☐ Connect with a friend or family member
- ☐ Help others
- ☐ Go to the doctor for a check-up
- ☐ Journal
- ☐ Pet a furry friend
- ☐ Meditate
- ☐ Practice guided imagery
- ☐ Start therapy
- ☐ Read
- ☐ Take a nap
- ☐ Watch a movie or TV show
- ☐ Listen to music
- ☐ Do something creative (e.g., draw, paint, color)

Now, go back and look at that list. What items did you not check off? What new activities do you need to add to your self-care practice? If your basic needs–like eating regularly, staying hydrated, and sleeping–are not being met, be sure to make them a priority starting now. Grieving requires a tremendous amount of energy, stamina, and strength, so you need to be properly fueled and rested up to do it!

My Self-Care Plan

Below is a self-care template. In each of the blank spaces, write down all of the self-care activities that you will do to nurture your health and well-being as you grieve.

Physical (Body)

Emotional (Mind)
Spiritual (Spirit)

Coping Skills

When faced with a distressing scenario, people often use tools and techniques known as *coping skills* to deal with the situation and the challenges that it brings. Although coping skills fall under the umbrella of self-care, there is a slight difference between the two concepts.

Coping skills, on the one hand, are the things that we do in the present moment during a difficult situation to manage the distressing thoughts and feelings we are experiencing. They can help calm us down, manage our emotions, or cheer us up. Self-care, on the other hand, refers to the broader range of tools and techniques that we use on a regular basis to maintain our emotional well-being.

Just like self-care, coping skills are a necessity during the grieving process. If they are not in place, you are more likely to experience deep depression and prolonged grief following the loss of your loved one.

Whether or not you realize it, you already possess a set of skills that you use regularly to deal with stressful or unpleasant thoughts and emotions. As you process the loss of your loved one, you may be able to use these previously acquired skills to manage your grief–and you may even pick up some additional new skills along the way.

In the same way that grieving is an individual process, your coping skillset will be unique to you and your situation. What works for one person may not work for another. Figuring out what strategies work best for you during distressing situations and making use of those tools is essential during this process. It is also crucial that you are patient with yourself as you experiment with various coping skills, because a particular technique or tool may work wonders in one context but be ineffective in another.

Below is a list of coping skills that you may find helpful as you grieve the loss of your loved one.

- Complete a puzzle
- Read a book
- Paint or draw
- Do a crossword puzzle, seek & find, or sudoku
- Watch a movie or TV show
- Watch YouTube videos
- Journal or write
- Exercise
- Make arts and crafts
- Use your senses to ground yourself:
  - Find something to touch
  - Notice what you see around you
  - Smell some things around you
  - Notice what you hear around you
- Breathe deeply for a few minutes
- Use a fidget toy
- Count backwards from 20
- Move your body
- Do yoga

- Practice guided imagery, meditation, or visualization
- Make a gratitude list
- Write a list of goals
- Write a list of personal strengths
- Keep an inspirational quote with you (e.g., on your phone lock screen, in your wallet)
- Call a friend or someone you trust
- Encourage others
- Set boundaries and say no
- Join a support group
- Spend time with friends and/or family
- Serve someone in need

Exercise: Coping Skills Toolbox

What's in Your Toolbox

A Coping Skills Toolbox is a place for you to keep all of the tools and techniques that you use to calm yourself down when feeling distressed. It is much easier to remember all of the tools you have if they are gathered in one place. Using the list of coping skills from the previous section as a guide, compile your own list of coping skills that you can use throughout the grieving process in the box below. Feel free to write down any tools or techniques not included in the previous section's list that you have used before and have found to be helpful.

MY COPING SKILLS TOOLBOX

The New Normal

After losing someone to suicide, you and your world will never be quite the same again. What you once saw as your normal way of life is completely obliterated by the tremendous confusion, sadness, and pain you feel in the wake of your loved one's death. While the grieving process looks different for everyone, there are a number of thoughts, feelings, and behaviors that are common amongst those bereaved by suicide. These shared experiences are all a part of what is often called "the new normal"—the new way of life that survivors must adjust to after losing their loved one to suicide.

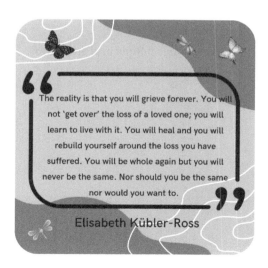

The reality is that you will grieve forever. You will not 'get over' the loss of a loved one; you will learn to live with it. You will heal and you will rebuild yourself around the loss you have suffered. You will be whole again but you will never be the same. Nor should you be the same nor would you want to.

Elisabeth Kübler-Ross

Exercise:

Below is a list of thoughts, feelings, and experiences that may be a part of your new normal. Take your time to read through the list, checking off all of the things that you yourself have experienced.

- ☐ Sudden painful memories or reminders of loved one (i.e., flashbacks)
- ☐ Lack of support from others
- ☐ Insensitive remarks by others
- ☐ Feelings of guilt and blame
- ☐ Intense feelings at holidays, birthdays, anniversaries, and/or other special occasions
- ☐ Negative emotions about feeling positive
- ☐ Resurfacing emotions, thoughts, and memories
- ☐ Suicidal thoughts
- ☐ Not remembering certain things (i.e. selective memory)
- ☐ The search for "*Why?*"
- ☐ Fear of other people leaving or dying
- ☐ Fear of ghosts or spirits
- ☐ Difficulty trusting other people and situations

Grief is a Journey

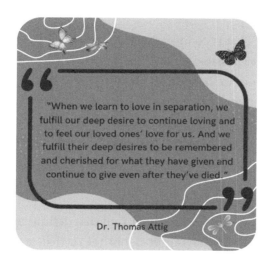

"When we learn to love in separation, we fulfill our deep desire to continue loving and to feel our loved ones' love for us. And we fulfill their deep desires to be remembered and cherished for what they have given and continue to give even after they've died."

Dr. Thomas Attig

As human beings, we have an innate tendency to view our lives through a narrative lens, spinning everything that happens to us into a story with a beginning, middle, and end. We do this, in part, because it makes even the most difficult and painful situations bearable by giving us hope that there is an end in sight. We are particularly drawn to finding closure or resolution in situations because it helps us to see an experience as being a part of the past, which, in turn, allows us to find meaning in it and move on with our lives.

When it comes to grief, however, finding closure is not really an option. No matter how hard you try or how much time goes by, you will never "get over" the loss of your loved one. There will never come a day when you take one last step across the metaphorical finish line of your grieving journey, when you can say, "Okay, I'm finally done grieving."

Now, I know this might sound scary, but when you really think about it, it actually makes sense. How could you possibly get over someone who meant so much to you? How could you ever stop thinking about someone who had such a tremendous impact on your life? How could you possibly replace the unique relationship that you had with your loved one? The simple answer to these questions is that you can't–and you won't!

But guess what? That is completely normal and okay. No one who loses a loved one can ever possibly get over their grief. The relationships you form with people are not exchangeable, and the love you have for others is not temporary. When you lose a loved one, then, the role that they played in your life will never fully be replaced, and the love you had for them will never disappear. In fact, that love lives on in, and is often expressed through grief and mourning. And if you love someone deeply, you will grieve for them deeply.

That said, just because you will never find that definitive closure for your grief that you may be craving does not mean that you are doomed to live a sad and empty life. Rather, you can work towards reconciling with your grief. As psychologist and grief expert Dr. Alan Wolfet explains, "Reconciling our grief means integrating our new reality of a life without the physical presence of the person who died. Not just surviving, but really living, even thriving." Although grief reconciliation is incredibly beneficial, it is important to note that the process will not be easy, as it will show you just how strikingly different life is without your loved one. As you begin to adapt to this new reality on a cognitive, spiritual, physical, and emotional level, however, you will start to notice yourself more frequently laughing and smiling, doing the things that you used to love to do, and staying present in the moment. By reconciling with your grief in this way, you will learn how to find joy and peace in this new stage of life that you are in.

Signs of Reconciliation

Just like the overall grieving process, grief reconciliation is an individual experience that differs from person to person. That said, there are a number of experiences that those who are reconciling with their grief commonly go through, some of which are listed below:

- Acknowledging the reality and finality of the death.
- Allowing yourself to fully embrace the pain of your loss.
- Establishing a new self-identity and living life in your new normal without your loved one.
- Adjusting to the new role changes that have come as a result of your loss.
- Returning to normal sleeping and eating habits.
- Finding pleasure in experiences that you used to enjoy before your loss.
- Establishing new and healthy relationships.
- Living life without guilt.
- Gaining insight that you don't "get over" grief rather, you find meaning and purpose in life.
- Feeling driven to organize and plan for your future.
- Finding safe ways to express and manage your grief.
- Developing and utilizing a support system of people who can help you through your grief journey.
- Welcome change in your life.
- Accepting that the pain of loss is a natural part of life that comes from your capacity to give and receive love.

PART II

Learning to Live with Grief

> How lucky I am to have something that makes saying goodbye so hard.
>
> A.A. Milne,
> The Complete Tales of Winnie-the-Pooh

As I said many times in Part I of this journal, grief is a personal experience. While there are particular emotions, thoughts, physical feelings, and behavioral reactions that people often experience as a result of grief, the overall grieving process varies based on the individual, their scenario, and their relationship with their loved one.

As you go through the grieving process, it is incredibly important that you take the time to notice and reflect on the things you are feeling, thinking, and doing. Thus, the primary purpose of Part II is to give you a place to document your personal grief journey in this way, as well as to allow you to remember the life of your loved one. In it, you will find a range of journal prompts, coping tips, and blank pages that are meant to help you work through your grief in a healthy way. That said, there is no one correct way to do this work. Rather, in the same way that grief is unique to the individual experiencing it, this journal can be used in whatever way you find to be most helpful. So whether you prefer to write, paste personal photographs, doodle, paint, or create a magazine collage, I encourage you to do what feels right to you.

Past Losses

While you may not realize it, you likely have experienced many losses over the course of your lifetime. In fact, we all have! Loss of a job, pet, relationship, childhood, or dreams are just a few examples of these past losses that oftentimes get swept under the rug and, consequently, go unnoticed for long periods of time.

That said, your past shapes how you experience and understand your present, so your past losses may have started to resurface in the wake of your most recent loss–the loss of your loved one. In addition to the pain that they may be causing you on their own, these past losses also may be increasing the severity of your reaction to the present loss of your loved one. This is, in part, due to the fact that the recent death of your loved one may be bringing up feelings and thoughts related to these past losses of yours, making for an even more complicated grieving process.

Loss History

One method you can use to identify your past losses and their impact on you is creating a loss history timeline. By exploring your past losses in a chronological manner, you will come to know the ways that loss has affected you both in the past and in the present. Additionally, creating a loss timeline will give you the opportunity to see what your past coping mechanisms and support systems were, as well as to learn how they may be able to help you grieve in the present.

In the space provided below, create your own loss timeline. Above the line, list your losses and the dates on which they occurred in chronological order. These losses can be any events where you felt that you lost something important to you, whether that be a break-up with a romantic partner, the death of a pet, termination from a job, or the development of a chronic illness. Below the line, describe the feelings you had at the time of each loss.

You can use the following example of a loss timeline to help you create your own:

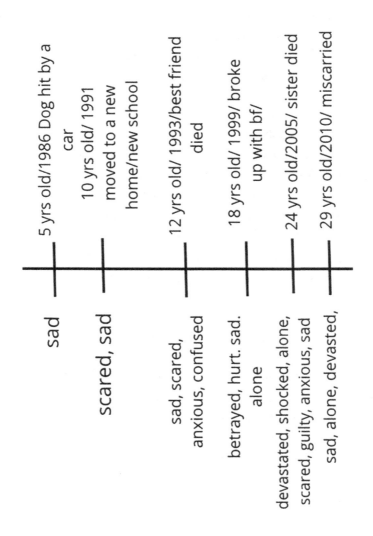

Loss Line

Now that you have completed your loss timeline, use the following chart to reflect on how you coped with the losses you listed above, the support systems you had at the time, and the emotions that come up when you think about each loss.

Loss/Date	Feelings	How did you cope?	What were your support systems?	Present day feelings?

While identifying and reflecting on past losses is a crucial part of the grieving journey, it is definitely not easy work. Consequently, doing this exercise may have caused you to experience unpleasant or painful thoughts and emotions. If this is the case, use the space below to reflect on any particular past losses that triggered you in this way. Notice the specific thoughts and feelings you are having as you think about these losses, and try your best to describe what you are experiencing.

_____

_____

_____

_____

_____

_____

_____

_____

Snowball Effect

Each loss you have experienced throughout your life is like a single snowflake. In the same way that tiny snowflakes can begin to pile up and eventually become a massive snowball, your losses–when not appropriately felt, expressed, and dealt with–can slowly grow into a bigger and bigger burden that feels heavier with each additional loss you experience. This phenomenon is known as the Snowball Effect.

In the following exercise, you will explore how your past losses have accumulated over time, creating an ever-growing "snowball" of loss and grief.

Below is an example of the snowball effect:

Parents broke up

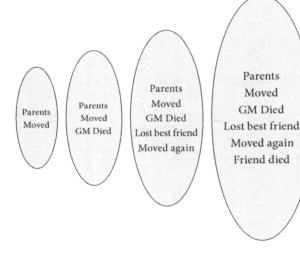

Parents
Moved

Parents
Moved
GM Died

Parents
Moved
GM Died
Lost best friend
Moved again

Parents
Moved
GM Died
Lost best friend
Moved again
Friend died

Parents
Moved
GM Died
Lost best friend
Moved again
Friend Died
Break-up
Dad died

GM died

Using the diagram below write down your individual losses in each of the circles in chronological order, moving left to right, that have accumulated over time.

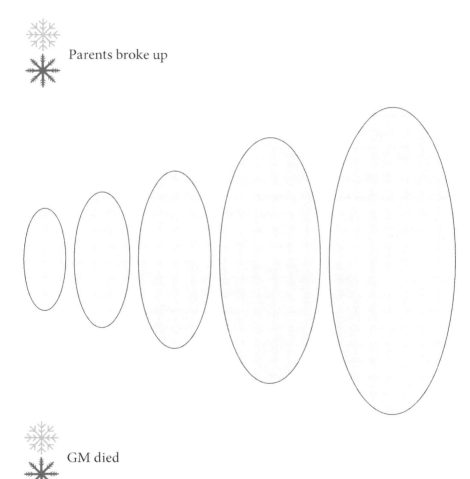

Parents broke up

GM died

The Reality of Loss

The first major undertaking in the grief journey is to become fully aware of, and accept that, the loss that you are grieving has occurred. Hearing the news that someone you loved has died is an incredibly shocking and painful experience, and those first few days and weeks following it are no easier. It can be remarkably difficult to process something so life-altering, especially as you attempt to mourn your loved one, identify your support system, and generally make sense of this new reality that you have been thrust into.

Blessed are those who mourn, for they shall be comforted.

Matthew 5:4

Life of My Loved One

The following activity is intended to help you start to tell the story of your loved one. In the spaces below, share some of their characteristics, accomplishments, and important milestones.

The name of my loved one who died is

_____

(Name of loved one)

_____ was born on _____.

(Name of loved one)

The date _____ died is _____.

(Name of loved one)

_____ was _____ years old

(Name of loved one)

Your greatest accomplishments were:

_____

_____

_____

_____

_____

You were known for:

_____

_____

_____

_____

_____

Three of your greatest strengths were:

_____

_____

_____

_____

_____

Some of your important milestones were:

_____

_____

_____

_____

_____

My favorite picture of you is:

Hearing the News

Some people can remember exactly where they were at, what they were wearing, and what they were doing when they heard that their loved one had passed. Others cannot remember anything about that moment, having gone into a state of shock the second they heard the news.

Telling someone that their loved one has died is a challenging and stressful task that requires tremendous sensitivity. Unfortunately, the news is not always delivered in a careful, sensitive manner. This can leave the person receiving the news with secondary trauma, which can further complicate their already difficult grieving process.

For instance, it is not uncommon for bereaved individuals to find out that their loved one has died via social media before their family or friends have the chance to tell them. While people frequently use social media as a means of expressing their sympathies in the wake of a death, they sometimes do so without thinking about the devastating impact that their posts can have on others. As a result, a seemingly innocent and well-intentioned post can easily become a source of trauma for the deceased's family members and close friends who have not yet been notified of their death.

In the space below, write about how you found out about your loved one's death.

I learned of your passing from …

_____

When I heard the news of your death, I felt …

_____

_____

_____

_____

_____

_____

My immediate reaction after hearing the news was …

_____

_____

_____

_____

_____

The way I was told about your death left me feeling and thinking …

_____

_____

_____

_____

_____

The Funeral

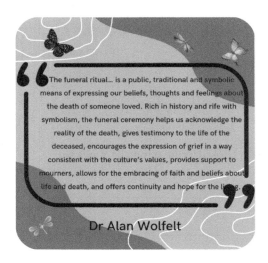

"The funeral ritual... is a public, traditional and symbolic means of expressing our beliefs, thoughts and feelings about the death of someone loved. Rich in history and rife with symbolism, the funeral ceremony helps us acknowledge the reality of the death, gives testimony to the life of the deceased, encourages the expression of grief in a way consistent with the culture's values, provides support to mourners, allows for the embracing of faith and beliefs about life and death, and offers continuity and hope for the living."

Dr Alan Wolfelt

Funerals, memorials, and life celebrations are an important part of the grieving process, as they help those who have lost a loved one come to terms with the death. These events are a time for the bereaved to pay tribute to their loved one while also getting the love and support they need from their family and friends.

In the space provided below, describe your experience with the funeral, memorial service, or life celebration that was held for your loved one.

Type of service (e.g., funeral, memorial, life celebration): _____

Date of the service: _____

Place the service was held: _____

The first time I saw their body, I ...

_____

_____

... and I felt ...

_____

_____

_____

My involvement in the service was ...

_____

_____

_____

What I remember most about that day is ...

_____

_____

_____

_____

On that day, I wish I would have ...

_____

_____

_____

_____

_____

_____

_____

_____

_____

_____

Honoring Key Dates

Use this page as a place to write down and store any important dates related to your loved one. Remember: there is no right or wrong way to spend these key dates. Just as your grief journey is unique to you, the way in which you choose to spend these days is your choice. On these key dates, you may want to do something special to honor your loved one, like baking their favorite dessert or buying their favorite flowers. Or you may just want to ignore the day and stay in bed the entire time. Whatever you choose is absolutely fine. You should also make a conscious effort to be kind, gentle, and patient with yourself whenever these key dates arrive, as you likely will be more emotional around those times.

Anniversary of your death:_____

Your birthday: _____

Wedding or engagement anniversary: _____

Special holidays:

_____

_____

_____

_____

_____

_____

Other significant dates (e.g., day we first met, day you graduated or would have graduated, day we bought our first house):

_____

_____

_____

_____

_____

_____

_____

_____

Rituals

Rituals are symbolic, repeated actions that help you stay connected to things that are important to you, such as your community, a higher power, or another human being. In times of grief, rituals can be particularly comforting for those who have lost a loved one, as they are a wonderful outlet for expressing the complicated thoughts and feelings that come in the wake of a death. They also can help grieving individuals find solace, stability, and purpose in the unpredictable chaos that often follows the passing of a loved one. Grieving rituals do not have to follow any set of rules in order to be beneficial–they just have to be meaningful to the individual practicing them. Some examples of the various rituals I have come across are lighting candles or releasing balloons on the anniversary of a loved one's death, cooking a loved one's favorite meal, or visiting a loved one's gravesite on their birthday.

In the space below, list some of the grieving rituals you practice that are meaningful to you:

_____

_____

_____

_____

_____

_____

_____

What new rituals can you start practicing to remember and honor your loved one? Are there any important dates (e.g., your loved one's favorite holiday, their birthday) when you can practice any of these new rituals?:

_____

_____

_____

_____

_____

_____

_____

Support System

During this time of grief, it is crucial that you have an accessible support system made up of caring, loving, and trustworthy individuals. These people should be willing and able to provide you with the emotional support, strength, and wisdom that you need throughout your grieving journey.

As you process the loss of your loved one, you may find yourself feeling overwhelmed, lost, and confused. At times, you may need help completing household tasks, or you may just need someone to talk to. It is in situations like these that you should reach out to the people in your support system and ask them for help.

Whether or not you realize it, many people want to be there for you as you grieve, but they do not know how to help. It is important, then, that you communicate with them–let them know how they can be there for you.

Below are questions intended to help you examine the support system you had at the time of your loss, as well as to help you build a stronger support system as you move forward in your grieving journey.

Who was there to support you in the first few hours, days, and weeks following your loss?

_____

_____

_____

_____

_____

What did they do that was helpful to you?

_____

_____

_____

_____

_____

_____

What did they do (or not do) that was *not* so helpful to you?

_____

_____

_____

_____

_____

Now is a good time to reexamine your current support system. This will help you create a grief support system.

Name three people you are comfortable talking to about your grief.

1.
2.
3.

Who is in your support system in the present moment? You can list any individuals, groups, and communities that are helping you through your grieving journey.

_____

_____

_____

_____

_____

In what specific ways have those whom you listed above helped you thus far? In what additional ways could they help you going forward?

_____

_____

_____

_____

_____

_____

The feeling of isolation that often comes with grief can make it difficult to identify the individuals and groups around you who would gladly become a part of your support system if you simply let them know how they could help you. Take some time to think about, and list, the people and communities in your life who can provide you with additional support as you grieve.

_____

_____

_____

_____

_____

_____

Describing Grief

Grief has a funny way of sneaking up on you when you least expect it. Perhaps it shows up when you hear your loved one's favorite song on the radio. Or maybe it comes when you see someone of the same age, height, and hair color as your loved one at the store. It could even be something as simple as meeting someone with the same name as your loved one that triggers a sudden pang of grief. At first, these sudden onslaughts of grief can feel excruciating. As you make your way further along in your grief journey, however, you will learn to more accurately anticipate and manage these grief-driven reactions so that they do not feel so shocking and intense when they occur.

In the following few pages, you will find prompts intended to help you document and reflect on what your grief feels and looks like to you.

What My Grief Looks Like

For some people, talking about the death of their loved one is incredibly difficult–so difficult, in fact, that they seek out other ways to express their grief. One example of these alternative means of grief expression is art. Art offers bereaved individuals a unique avenue to process, convey, and manage their grief responses without needing to put their confusing and painful experience into words. Whether it is painting, drawing, sculpting, collaging, or any other artistic medium, the creative expression of art allows people to open themselves up and release the grief that they have been holding inside.

In the space provided below, take a few moments to create a visual representation of **what your grief looked like when the loss first occurred**. You can draw whatever images and write whatever words come to mind when you think about that initial feeling of grief. You can even cut out pictures from newspapers and magazines to make a collage that represents what your grief first felt like. Use whatever creative means you feel is most helpful.

Now, create an image of **what your grief looks like in the present moment.**

Grief is Like _____

Sometimes, it might feel impossible to put into words what your grief feels like. You may even struggle to explain how and what you are feeling, in general. That said, metaphors are a tremendously useful tool for describing grief and emotions. For instance, you can say, "Grief is like a hurricane," or, "Grief is like a roller coaster."

What metaphor(s) best describe your grief?

_____

_____

_____

_____

_____

QUICK TIP

Simple Grounding Techniques

**If you find yourself anxious
take a deep breath and identify and describe:**

**5 THINGS THAT YOU SEE
4 THINGS THAT YOU CAN FEEL OR TOUCH
3 THINGS THAT YOU CAN HEAR
2 THINGS THAT YOU CAN SMELL
1 THING YOU CAN TASTE**

Grief is Like a Wave

As you make your way through the grieving journey, you will have times when your emotions suddenly come crashing down on you like a wave. Some of those waves will momentarily shake your balance and make you feel unsteady. Others will completely knock you off of your feet and pull you under water with them. When these waves of grief hit, you may feel like you are drowning in feelings of sadness, anger, guilt, and anxiety with seemingly no way to resurface and take a breath of air.

When you are hit with a wave of grief, what do you feel like? What specific emotions do you experience?

_____

_____

_____

_____

_____

_____

_____

_____

_____

_____

_____

Write about a time when it felt like a wave of grief came crashing down on you out of nowhere. Where were you? What were you doing? What emotions did you feel? How did you react?

_____

_____

_____

_____

_____

_____

_____

_____

_____

_____

_____

_____

_____

_____

_____

_____

Sometimes these waves of grief come at a slow and steady pace, giving you a chance to come up for air every once in a while to gather yourself before the next wave hits. Other times, however, these waves come quickly and unexpectedly, pulling you into a rip current of grief that leaves you tossing and turning in a whirlpool of emotions. Next time you feel yourself getting pulled into one of these grief rip currents, do the following four things in order to break free from its grip.

GRIEF CURRENTS

Know your options

IF CAUGHT IN A GRIEF CURRENT

1. Remember whatever you are feeling, it will eventually pass.
2. Focus on your breathing and take deep breaths.
3. Just "float" and go with the feelings.
4. If you need help or need to talk to someone, call someone in your support circle.

Emotions

The variety of emotions that come with grief can be incredibly overwhelming, confusing, and difficult to navigate. Anger, sadness, fear, and guilt are some of the most common emotions associated with grief, but there are countless others that you may experience as you make your way through your grieving journey. In the following several pages, you will have the opportunity to explore your experience with these different emotions following the loss of your loved one.

QUICK TIP

Calming Your Body

PRACTICE GROUNDING:

RUN YOUR HANDS UNDER COLD WATER

FEEL YOUR FEET ON THE GROUND

TOUCH OBJECTS AROUND YOU

PUT A COOL CLOTH ON YOUR FOREHEAD

Anger

I feel like I am being consumed by anger right now. I am so angry about ...

_____

_____

_____

_____

_____

_____

_____

_____

_____

_____

_____

_____

_____

_____

When I get angry, I ...

_____

_____

_____

_____

_____

_____

_____

_____

_____

_____

_____

_____

_____

_____

_____

_____

Guilt

I am overwhelmed with guilt. I feel guilty about …

_____

_____

_____

_____

_____

_____

_____

_____

_____

_____

_____

_____

_____

_____

_____

_____

Fear

I have become fearful of so many things since you've been gone. Some of the fears I have are …

_____

_____

_____

_____

_____

_____

_____

_____

_____

_____

_____

_____

_____

Sadness

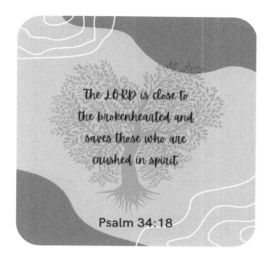

The LORD is close to the brokenhearted and saves those who are crushed in spirit

Psalm 34:18

Today, I feel sad because …

_____

_____

_____

_____

_____

_____

_____

_____

_____

_____

I feel saddest when …

_____

_____

_____

_____

_____

_____

_____

_____

_____

_____

_____

_____

_____

_____

_____

_____

_____

_____

I Feel Afraid

Today, I felt afraid when …

_____

_____

_____

_____

_____

_____

_____

If you were here, I think you would tell me …

_____

_____

_____

_____

_____

_____

_____

_____

Loneliness

Since you've been gone, I have felt incredibly lonely. Even though others around me are grieving, as well, I feel as if I am all alone. I feel most alone when ...

_____

_____

_____

_____

_____

_____

_____

_____

_____

_____

_____

_____

_____

Favorites

Over the next few pages, you will have the chance to share some of your and your loved one's favorite things. If you cannot remember some of your loved one's favorites, do no worry! I encourage you to reach out to family members and friends who may know the correct answer, because it may open the door to a much-needed conversation about your loved one.

Some of Our Favorites

My favorite color: _____

Your favorite color: _____

My favorite movie: _____

Your favorite movie: _____

My favorite TV show: _____

Your favorite TV show: _____

My favorite actor: _____

Your favorite actor: _____

My favorite food: _____

Your favorite food: _____

My favorite ice cream flavor: _____

Your favorite ice cream flavor: _____

My favorite animal: _____

Your favorite animal: _____

My favorite way to relax: _____

Your favorite way to relax: _____

My favorite song: _____

Your favorite song: _____

My favorite musical artist or group: _____

Your favorite musical artist or group: _____

My favorite vacation spot: _____

Your favorite vacation spot: _____

My favorite holiday: _____

Your favorite holiday: _____

My favorite: _____

Your favorite: _____

My favorite: _____

Your favorite: _____

My favorite: _____

Your favorite: _____

My favorite: _____

Your favorite: _____

My favorite: _____

Your favorite: _____

More Favorites

Some of my favorite stories about you are …

_____

_____

_____

_____

_____

_____

_____

_____

_____

_____

My favorite holiday memory with you is ...

_____

_____

_____

_____

_____

My favorite gift you gave me was ...

_____

_____

_____

_____

_____

The best gift I gave you was ...

_____

_____

_____

_____

_____

Some of My Favorite Pictures of You

Some of My Favorite Pictures of Us

Working Through the Pain

> The cure for pain
> is in the pain.
>
> Rumi

Generally speaking, losing a loved one is a remarkably painful experience. That said, some moments feel worse than others, especially when emotions like regret and remorse come to the surface. Rest assured, though, that these particularly painful moments are a completely normal part of the grieving process. Although it can be hard to see the light at the end of the tunnel when you are in the midst of an emotionally trying time, I promise that you will make it to the other side–you just have to let yourself actually feel the emotions that come up and work through them.

In the next few pages, you will have the chance to reflect on some of the particularly painful experiences that you have had during your grieving journey.

The Empty Chair

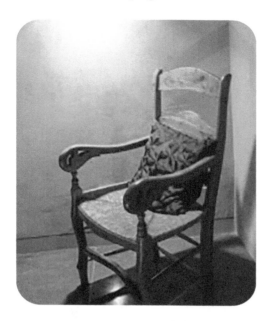

The kitchen stands at the heart of the home, serving as a focal point for the people who live there. Throughout the day, family and friends gather around the kitchen table to share a meal and catch each other up on their days. It is in that room and at that table that so many stories are told and so many memories are made. When a loved one dies, however, the empty chair that they leave at the kitchen table can make this room that was once filled with laughter, warmth, and love feel lifeless, cold, and vacant.

You may be familiar with this painful feeling that comes when you look at the empty spot where your loved one used to sit at the kitchen table. Or maybe you experience it when you walk past the couch they used to lounge on in the living room or the rocking chair they used to sit in on the porch. Wherever it may be, the seemingly harmless empty seat where your loved one once sat can easily trigger a wave of grief-related emotions to come crashing down on you.

In the space below, write, draw, or collage about your experience with seeing the empty spot where your loved one used to sit.

_____

_____

_____

_____

_____

Unfinished Business

There are so many things that I didn't get to say to you before you died.

I wish I could have said …

_____

_____

_____

_____

_____

_____

_____

_____

If I had the chance to say these things to you, I imagine you would say to me ...

_____

_____

_____

_____

_____

_____

_____

_____

_____

_____

_____

_____

_____

_____

_____

Would've, Could've, Should've

When you were still here with me, I wish I would have …

_____

_____

_____

_____

_____

_____

When you were still alive, I should have …

_____

_____

_____

_____

_____

_____

_____

Something I could have done better while you were still here with me is ...

_____

_____

_____

_____

_____

_____

_____

If I could ask you one question, it would be ...

_____

_____

_____

_____

_____

_____

_____

Regret

Some days, I feel so full of regret for the things I did and the things I didn't do while you were still here with me. A few of the regrets I have are …

_____

_____

_____

_____

_____

_____

_____

_____

_____

_____

_____

_____

_____

_____

_____

I'm Sorry

I am sorry for …

_____

_____

_____

_____

_____

In the space below, write a letter to your loved one expressing your remorse.

_____

_____

_____

_____

_____

_____

_____

_____

_____

_____

Memories

In the following few pages, you will have the opportunity to reflect on some of the memories you have of your loved one. Even after you complete the prompts, you can come back to this section whenever you are missing your loved one to remember the hilarious conversations you had, the secrets you shared, the challenging situations you endured, and the crazy adventures you went on with them.

I Will Always Remember

I will always remember the time when you …

_____

_____

_____

_____

_____

_____

_____

I will always remember that you …

_____

_____

_____

_____

_____

_____

_____

I will always remember when we talked about …

_____

_____

_____

_____

_____

_____

_____

Good Times

Some of the funniest memories I have of you are …

_____

_____

_____

_____

_____

_____

_____

I remember laughing with you about …

_____

_____

_____

_____

_____

_____

_____

_____

_____

_____

_____

_____

_____

_____

_____

Honoring Your Memory

Honoring your loved one's memory and keeping their legacy alive is a vital part of your grieving journey. That said, there is no one right way to do this—the way in which you choose to honor your loved one is completely up to you. It is important, then, that you find ways to honor them that feel good to you. Telling the story of your loved one, holding a mass in their name, donating to a cause they supported, or planting a tree in their memory are just a few examples of ways that you can honor your loved one and keep their legacy alive.

Some of the ways that I have honored your memory are …

_____

_____

_____

_____

_____

_____

_____

_____

_____

_____

_____

_____

Today, I will keep your memory alive by …

_____

_____

_____

_____

_____

_____

Other ways I will honor your memory in the future are …

_____

_____

_____

_____

_____

_____

_____

Appreciation

What I appreciate about you is …

_____

_____

_____

_____

_____

_____

_____

I want to thank you for …

_____

_____

_____

_____

_____

_____

_____

More Memories

Those who were always there for us in this life will always be there for us in our memories.

I remember when you and I …

_____

_____

_____

_____

_____

_____

_____

_____

_____

_____

My happiest memory of you is ...

_____

_____

_____

_____

_____

_____

_____

I don't ever want to forget …

_____

_____

_____

_____

_____

_____

_____

_____

Music

> " When you're happy, you enjoy the music. But, when you're sad, you understand the lyrics. "
>
> Frank Ocean

We have all heard the saying, "Music is good for the soul"—and believe it or not, this is actually based in some truth! In fact, research has shown that listening to music can reduce stress and improve your mood.

When you are grieving, then, listening to music can help create a safe space for you to feel, process, and express the variety of emotions you are experiencing. Music can also help you remember, connect with, and honor your loved one as you grieve.

Whenever I hear the song/artist, I think of you because ...

_____

_____

_____

_____

_____

Whenever I listen to that song/artist, I feel ...

_____

_____

_____

_____

_____

_____

_____

Some days, I just need to remember you, so I listen to ...

_____

_____

_____

_____

_____

_____

_____

_____

In the space below, create a playlist that reminds you of your loved one and makes you feel good:

_____

_____

_____

_____

_____

_____

_____

_____

_____

_____

_____

_____

_____

_____

_____

Rough Days

Belly Breathing

BELLY BREATHING IS A QUICK WAY TO CALM YOUR BODY DOWN. START BY PUTTING YOUR HANDS ON YOUR BELLY & IMAGINING A BALLOON IS IN THERE. TAKE A SLOW, DEEP BREATH IN YOUR NOSE, FILLING THE BALLOON ALL THE WAY UP. YOU WILL FEEL YOUR BELLY BEGIN TO EXPAND AS YOU DO THIS. THEN, SLOWLY BREATH OUT YOUR MOUTH, FEELING THE IMAGINARY BALLOON SHRINK. REPEAT THIS FOR 1-2 MINUTES."

While grieving the loss of a loved one is an overall difficult thing to do, some days are bound to be more challenging than others. Maybe you cannot focus on work or school because your thoughts are racing a mile a minute. Maybe you have to make a decision and could really use your loved one's advice. Maybe you just want someone to talk to but feel like no one in your life understands what you are going through. There are an infinite number of variables that can make certain days more painful than others as you grieve, and all of them are completely valid. When you are having one of these rough days, it is important to remember that these ups and downs are a natural part of the grieving process.

Over the next few pages, you will have the opportunity to reflect on some of the rough days that you have had on your grieving journey.

I Need Advice

Right now, I could really use your advice about …

_____

_____

_____

_____

_____

_____

If you were here with me right now, I imagine you would say ...

_____

_____

_____

_____

_____

_____

_____

Tough Time

Today, I am having a really tough time with …

_____

_____

_____

_____

_____

_____

_____

What I need to hear from you right now is …

_____

_____

_____

_____

_____

_____

_____

_____

In order to soothe and comfort myself today, I did …

_____

_____

_____

_____

_____

_____

_____

_____

_____

_____

Come to Me, all you who labor and are heavy laden, and I will give you rest. Take My yoke upon you and learn from Me, for I am gentle and lowly in heart, and you will find rest for your souls. For My yoke is easy and My burden is light.

Matthew 11:28-30

Racing Thoughts

My mind is racing right now. The thoughts won't stop. Here are all of those thoughts:

_____

_____

_____

_____

_____

_____

_____

Ever since you passed, I can't get these specific thoughts, images, and memories out of my mind…

_____

_____

_____

_____

_____

_____

_____

No One Understands

No one seems to truly understand the pain that I am feeling right now. I wish they would ...

_____

_____

_____

_____

_____

_____

_____

_____

_____

_____

_____

_____

_____

_____

_____

_____

Holidays

After losing a loved one, holidays do not feel the same. It is incredibly difficult to watch everyone around you joyfully celebrating when you are grieving. Interestingly, the days leading up to a holiday are often more emotionally intense than the actual holiday, itself.

During the holidays, you may be tempted to numb yourself and hide away from everyone. If you prepare beforehand, however, holidays without your loved one do not have to be so terribly painful. Below are a few tips for how to make the holidays more bearable and even enjoyable.

1. **Honor old traditions**
    You can honor your loved one's memory by continuing to do some of their favorite traditions. Perhaps your grandmother cooked a special stuffing for Thanksgiving dinner or your husband loved to go to the local 4th of July parade. Whatever those traditions may be, you can honor your loved one by continuing to do them even after they have passed.

2. **Create new memories**
    While traditions are great, you should also allow yourself to do something completely different this year. You could have someone else host the family holiday party, you could try a new holiday dessert recipe, or you could hang up some new decorations–do whatever new thing you want to do, as long as it feels good to you. And if you find it difficult to make new memories without your loved one, just remember that they would want you to be enjoying the holidays.

3. **Plan ahead to fill the empty roles**

   After a loss, there are roles that your loved one once played in your holiday celebrations that will need to be filled. Maybe your dad always carved the Thanksgiving turkey, or your brother always hung up the Christmas lights. Planning ahead to make sure that someone else will take on those roles that your loved one once filled will help the holiday flow smoother and will make it less painful.

4. **Donate something to a cause that your loved one supported, or volunteer at a place that was special to them**

   By giving back and helping others, you can reduce your own sadness and anxiety while simultaneously bringing happiness to the life of someone else in need. This can be particularly challenging to do during the first year or two after losing a loved one. One idea I often suggest to people in this kind of situation is to purchase a gift that your loved one would have liked and donate it in their memory.

5. **Collect memories from friends and family members about your loved one and use them to create a memory book**

   During the holidays, you may run into a number of friends and family members who knew your loved one at get-togethers, parties, and other events. One way to go about putting together a memory book about your loved one, then, is to carry around a pen and some paper at these holiday gatherings and ask people there to share a memory of your loved one. You can also email family and friends and ask them to send you memories they have of your loved one. Write down, or print out, these memories and stick them in something like a box or a jar. (I have also suggested to clients that they put them in their loved one's stocking if it's Christmas.) In the privacy of your own home, and with people you feel comfortable with, take the time to read through each of these memories.

   Later, put these written or printed memories into a scrapbook, a photo album, or a notebook that you can look back on whenever you are missing your loved one.

Holidays Are Not the Same Without You

Today is _____.

The hardest thing about today was …

_____

_____

_____

_____

_____

What I missed most about spending this holiday with you was …

_____

_____

_____

_____

_____

_____

Something I did differently today was ...

_____

_____

_____

_____

_____

_____

_____

I kept your memory alive today by ...

_____

_____

_____

_____

_____

_____

_____

More Holidays Without You

My favorite _____ memory with you

(Name of Holiday)

is …

_____

_____

_____

_____

_____

The best present I received from you on a holiday was …

_____

_____

_____

_____

_____

_____

_____

_____

_____

I remember your favorite holiday was _____, because …

(Name of Holiday)

_____

_____

_____

_____

_____

_____

Your favorite thing to do during _____ was …

(Name of Holiday)

_____

_____

_____

_____

_____

_____

_____

Your favorite holiday tradition was …

_____

_____

_____

_____

_____

_____

Other holiday traditions that we had were …

_____

_____

_____

_____

_____

_____

_____

_____

_____

A holiday tradition I still keep now is …

_____

_____

_____

_____

_____

_____

_____

One way that I will keep your memory alive this _____ is …

(Name of Holiday)

_____

_____

_____

_____

_____

_____

_____

_____

It's Your Birthday

Today is your birthday. I really wish I could …

_____

_____

_____

_____

_____

_____

_____

Some of my favorite memories from your birthday are …

_____

_____

_____

_____

_____

_____

_____

My birthday message to you this year is …

_____

_____

_____

_____

_____

_____

_____

My favorite birthday picture(s) of you are …

_____

_____

_____

_____

_____

_____

_____

Letters to You

Throughout your grieving journey, there will be many times when you desperately want to talk to your loved one. Knowing that you can no longer sit at the dinner table and tell them about your terrible day or pick up the phone and ask them for their advice is one of the most painful things. In the next few pages of this journal, you will have the space to write some letters to your loved one about all of the things you wish you could tell them.

Dear _____,

(Name of Loved One)

_____

_____

_____

_____

_____

_____

_____

Dear _____,

(Name of Loved One)

_____

_____

_____

_____

_____

_____

_____

_____

_____

_____

_____

_____

_____

_____

_____

_____

_____

Dear _____,

_____

_____

_____

_____

_____

_____

_____

_____

_____

_____

_____

_____

_____

_____

_____

_____

_____

_____

Dear _____,

(Name of Loved One)

_____

_____

_____

_____

_____

_____

_____

_____

_____

_____

_____

_____

_____

_____

_____

_____

_____

_____

Dear _____,

(Name of Loved One)

_____

_____

_____

_____

_____

_____

_____

_____

_____

_____

_____

_____

_____

_____

_____

_____

_____

_____

Waves of Grief

At any moment of the day, the emotional pain of grief can come crashing down on you like a giant wave. Sometimes, the cause of the wave may be obvious (such as a picture of your loved one popping up on your social media timeline), so you are somewhat prepared for its impact. Other times, the wave may come seemingly out of nowhere, knocking you off of your feet without any warning. Throughout the next few pages, you will have the opportunity to reflect on some of your own experiences with these painful waves of grief, both expected and unexpected.

QUICK TIP

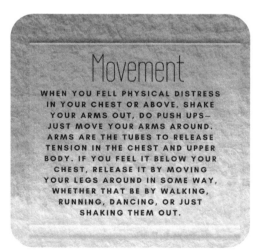

Movement

WHEN YOU FELL PHYSICAL DISTRESS IN YOUR CHEST OR ABOVE, SHAKE YOUR ARMS OUT, DO PUSH UPS— JUST MOVE YOUR ARMS AROUND. ARMS ARE THE TUBES TO RELEASE TENSION IN THE CHEST AND UPPER BODY. IF YOU FEEL IT BELOW YOUR CHEST, RELEASE IT BY MOVING YOUR LEGS AROUND IN SOME WAY, WHETHER THAT BE BY WALKING, RUNNING, DANCING, OR JUST SHAKING THEM OUT.

Lasts

The last time I saw you was …

_____

_____

_____

_____

_____

_____

The last memory I have of us together is …

_____

_____

_____

_____

_____

_____

_____

The last conversation we had was about …

_____

_____

_____

_____

_____

_____

_____

_____

_____

_____

_____

_____

_____

_____

_____

_____

_____

Bad Day

Today, I'm having a really bad day. I am feeling …

_____

_____

_____

_____

_____

_____

Today, I can't stop thinking about …

_____

_____

_____

_____

_____

_____

_____

Tears

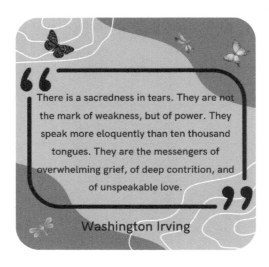

There is a sacredness in tears. They are not the mark of weakness, but of power. They speak more eloquently than ten thousand tongues. They are the messengers of overwhelming grief, of deep contrition, and of unspeakable love.

Washington Irving

Today, I couldn't stop crying …

_____

_____

_____

_____

_____

_____

_____

_____

_____

_____

Wanted You to Know

When good things happen to you or you experience something new, it is natural to want to share it with the ones you love. After losing a loved one, that does not change. Over the next few pages, you will be able to share about your good day, your special occasions, and your new experiences with your loved one.

Good Day

Something good happened today, and I wanted to share it with you.

_____

_____

_____

_____

_____

_____

_____

Something Special For You

Use this space to write a poem or song in memory of your loved one. You can also describe or draw something special that you did in their memory (e.g., getting a tattoo, donating to a special cause, planting a tree).

New Things

Since you've been gone, so many new things have entered my life. It feels so strange to meet these new people, to go to these new places, and to do these new activities without you here.

Some of the hardest new things I have had to do are …

_____

_____

_____

_____

_____

_____

_____

_____

_____

_____

_____

_____

_____

The first time I did _____
(New Experience)

without you I ...

_____

_____

_____

_____

_____

_____

_____

_____

_____

_____

_____

_____

_____

_____

_____

Special Occasion

Today was a special day. I wish you were here to celebrate with me. Let me tell you all about it.

_____

_____

_____

_____

_____

_____

_____

_____

_____

_____

_____

_____

_____

_____

Hard Times

God is our Refuge and strength, an ever present help in trouble.

Psalm 46:1

Grief is hard work, in general, but some of the obstacles you will face throughout your grieving journey will be more challenging than others. Some days, you may feel seen and supported by the people in your life, while other days, you may feel misunderstood and completely alone. Some days, you may be able to go about your regular life with some sense of normalcy, while other days, you may face constant reminders of your loved one that make your heart ache for them and their presence.

In the next few pages, you will have the chance to reflect on some of the particularly hard times that you have had during your grieving journey.

Things Better Left Unsaid

After losing a loved one, you may be subject to a host of unsolicited and insensitive remarks from others. Unfortunately, those kinds of comments are even more common for those who lost their loved one to suicide. Remarks like, "Didn't you know they were feeling that way?" or, "People who kill themselves are selfish," are examples of the terrible things that are often said to survivors. These inconsiderate, degrading, and hurtful words can easily weigh on you and break you down over time.

Below, you will have the chance to reflect on some of the times you were faced with insensitive comments made by others.

Recently, someone made a really insensitive comment to me. They said …

_____

_____

_____

_____

It caused me to feel …

_____

_____

_____

_____

_____

I responded by …

_____

_____

_____

_____

More Insensitive Remarks

Read through the following list of insensitive remarks commonly said to survivors and check off any of the ones that you yourself have heard after losing your loved one to suicide.

- ☐ Why would someone do something like that?
- ☐ Shouldn't you be over this by now?
- ☐ Didn't you know that they felt this way?
- ☐ You need to get over it.
- ☐ I know how you feel.
- ☐ It was their choice.
- ☐ That was a selfish decision.
- ☐ You have to let them go.
- ☐ Time will heal you.
- ☐ It was their time to go.
- ☐ They are in a better place now.
- ☐ Stop blaming yourself.
- ☐ Everything will be back to normal soon.
- ☐ There was nothing anyone could do.
- ☐ God gives you what you can handle.

It is important to note that although these kinds of comments are insensitive and have the potential to be incredibly hurtful, they are not always intended to be that way. While it may be hard to believe, most people who make these kinds of comments actually mean well when they say them. Of course, there are always going to be the selfish, mean-spirited people who make remarks with the intent to cause harm, but the majority of people really mean well by them.

Personally, it wasn't until after I lost my brother Jeff that I realized how some of the comments I myself had previously made in an attempt to be helpful were actually unintentionally hurtful. Some of the reasons why genuinely caring people may make inappropriate comments like this are:

1. They are uncomfortable with grief.
2. They want to comfort you.
3. They believe that by relating to your experience, they can help you feel connected to, and close with, them.
4. They are not well-informed on grief and suicide loss and, consequently, don't know any better.

Whenever you receive inconsiderate comments like this, you may find it helpful to take a step back and examine the intention behind them. In other words, try to think about what the person who made the comment actually meant to say and why they said it. By doing this, you will be disarming those hurtful and insensitive words, making your grieving journey just a bit easier.

I can endure all things through him who gives me strength

Philippians 4:13

Missing You

The thing I miss most about you is …

_____

_____

_____

_____

_____

_____

I miss how you used to …

_____

_____

_____

_____

_____

_____

_____

_____

Misunderstood

Now that you're gone, _____ just

(Name of person)

doesn't seem to understand that …

_____

_____

_____

_____

_____

_____

I really want to say to them …

_____

_____

_____

_____

_____

_____

_____

_____

I wish _____ would …

(Name of person)

_____

_____

_____

_____

_____

_____

One More Day

When you lose a loved one, you may find yourself yearning to have just one more day with them. If you had one more day with your loved one, how would you spend it? What would you do? What would you say?

If I had one more day with you …

_____

_____

_____

_____

_____

_____

Finding Hope

Losing a loved one to suicide is one of the most painful, life-altering experiences a person can go through. The way that it throws into question everything you once knew to be true about yourself and the world around you can easily put you in a state of despair. But I am here to tell you that it is, in fact, possible to find hope in the midst of your grief.

That hope may be sparked by something as simple as hearing someone recall a positive memory they have of your loved one, receiving a home-cooked meal from a friend, or seeing a butterfly in your garden. Whatever they may be, these small moments of hope can shift your perspective in a way that helps you realize that it is possible to go on living a life full of excitement, love, and joy without your loved one. Hope is an incredibly powerful force that can help you find comfort, strength, direction, and purpose amidst your grief.

In the next few pages, you will have the chance to reflect on your journey thus far to cope and find hope after the loss of your loved one.

Hopeful

Recently I saw _____, and it

(e.g., a rainbow, newspaper article, sunset)

gave me hope. This experience made me feel hopeful because …

_____

_____

_____

_____

_____

After seeing this, I changed my perspective on ...

_____

_____

_____

_____

Other experiences or things that help me feel hopeful are ...

_____

_____

_____

_____

_____

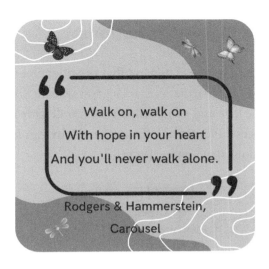

Walk on, walk on

With hope in your heart

And you'll never walk alone.

Rodgers & Hammerstein,
Carousel

I Am Coping

Some days, the pain is so overwhelming that it is hard to breathe, but I have found some ways to stay afloat.

I am learning to cope with your loss and release my pain by …

_____

_____

_____

_____

_____

_____

_____

Affirmations

An affirmation is a positive statement that provides emotional support or encouragement. Grief affirmations are a great way for you to take care of yourself using the love and compassion that you deserve and need during the grieving process. Practicing affirmations daily can help you manage the intense emotions that come with grief.

Grief Affirmations
My feelings matter.
I allow myself to feel this fully.
Today is for healing.
I am taking my time to grieve.
I am a survivor and I will get through this.
I grieve because I loved.
My grief will soften over time.
I take comfort in my memories.
The pain in my heart will heal.
I honor the love more than the loss.
I will honor you today by speaking your name.
I am gentle with myself as I heal.
When I bring myself to grief, it is healing.
I can hold on to my love and let go of my grief.

5 affirmations I can say daily are …

_____

_____

_____

_____

_____

Comfort

A comforting memory that I have about you is …

_____

_____

_____

_____

_____

_____

The people who are good at comforting me are …

_____

_____

_____

_____

_____

_____

_____

_____

Other things that comfort me are ...

_____

_____

_____

_____

_____

_____

Mending Piece by Piece

Although I may feel very different now that you're gone, I am mending myself, piece by piece. Using a lot of glue, I am slowly putting all my broken pieces back into place. Some of the ways I am rebuilding are ...

_____

_____

_____

_____

_____

_____

The glue that is helping me stay together is …

_____

_____

_____

_____

_____

_____

Living in the Present

I am learning to live in the present in the midst of my grief. Recently, I was able to experience pleasant emotions and enjoy the moment when …

_____

_____

_____

_____

_____

_____

Three things I can do to bring more joy into my life on a regular basis are ...

_____

_____

_____

_____

_____

_____

A Gift in My Grief

Throughout my career, many survivors have shared with me that it was while they were in the deepest depths of their grief that they found some of the greatest "gifts" in their loss. For instance, some have developed a strong sense of empathy for, and patience with, others after losing their loved one to suicide. Some have discovered a love for helping others after volunteering with an organization that their loved one used to work with. Others have forged an entirely new career path after having their perspective on life completely altered by their loss.

I know it may seem implausible to you at this very moment, but you, too, can find gifts like these as you move through your grief. Simply being aware that these little nuggets of hope are hidden throughout your grieving journey can make it easier to find them–so keep your eyes and heart open to the possibility! You did not choose to go through this extraordinarily painful experience of loss and grief, but you can choose to look for the blessings that are hidden in it.

Don't run away from grief, o' soul/ Look for the remedy inside the pain/ because the rose came from the thorn/ and the ruby came from a stone.

Rumi

A gift I have found during my grieving journey is …

_____

_____

_____

_____

_____

_____

_____

_____

_____

_____

_____

Even though you are not here with me, I have been able to keep certain gifts from our relationship. I am so thankful for them.

The gifts from our relationship that I will continue to cherish are …

_____

_____

_____

_____

_____

_____

_____

_____

_____

_____

_____

_____

_____

Lessons Learned

The greatest lesson I have learned from you is …

_____

_____

_____

_____

_____

_____

_____

_____

_____

_____

_____

_____

_____

_____

_____

_____

Always in My Heart

I am healing, and I will never forget you. You will always live in my heart. I am channeling my grief into something positive by ...

_____

_____

_____

_____

_____

_____

_____

_____

I Love You

I love you because …

_____

_____

_____

_____

_____

_____

_____

_____

_____

YOU CAN'T "GET OVER" SOMEONE WHO LIVES IN YOUR HEART

Resources

After a Suicide Resource Directory: Coping with Grief, Trauma, and Distress
http://www.personalgriefcoach.net/

Alliance of Hope for Suicide Survivors
https://allianceofhope.org/

American Association of Suicidology
https://suicidology.org/resources/suicide-loss-survivors/

American Foundation for Suicide Prevention
https://afsp.org/ive-lost-someone

Author's Website
https://www.lindafalascolcsw.com/

The Compassionate Friends
https://www.compassionatefriends.org/

Friends for Survival
https://friendsforsurvival.org/

Grief Share
https://www.griefshare.org/

National Suicide Prevention Lifeline
https://988lifeline.org/help-yourself/loss-survivors/

SAVE

https://save.org/what-we-do/grief-support/

Suicide Prevention Resource Center

www.sprc.org

Survivors of Suicide, Inc

http://www.sosphilly.org/

Tragedy Assistance Program for Survivors (TAPS)

https://www.taps.org/suicide

What's Your Grief

https://whatsyourgrief.com/resources/

References

Bolton, Iris, and Curtis Mitchell. *My Son--My Son--: A Guide to Healing After After Death, Loss Or Suicide*. Bolton Press, 1996.

Bolton, James M., Wendy Au, William D. Leslie, Patricia J. Martens, Murray W. Enns, Leslie L. Roos, Laurence Y. Katz et al. "Parents bereaved by offspring suicide: a population-based longitudinal case-control study." *JAMA psychiatry* 70, no. 2 (2013): 158-167.

Bush, Ashley Davis. *Transcending loss*. Penguin, 1997.

Centers for Disease Control and Prevention. "Grief and Loss." Last modified September 6, 2022. https://www.cdc.gov/mentalhealth/stress-coping/grief-loss/index.html.

Cerel, Julie, John R. Jordan, and Paul R. Duberstein. "The impact of suicide on the family." *Crisis: The Journal of Crisis Intervention and Suicide Prevention* 29, no. 1 (2008): 38.

Clark, Andrew. "Working with grieving adults." *Advances in Psychiatric Treatment* 10, no. 3 (2004): 164-170.

Doka, Kenneth J., and Terry L. Martin. *Men don't cry, women do: Transcending gender stereotypes of grief*. Routledge, 2014.

Dyregrov, Kari, and Atle Dyregrov. "Siblings after suicide—"The forgotten bereaved"." *Suicide and Life-Threatening Behavior* 35, no. 6 (2005): 714-724.

Fileva, Iskra. "Why We Seek Closure." Psychology Today, April 25, 2020. https://www.psychologytoday.com/us/blog/the-philosophers-diaries/202004/why-we-seek-closure.

Fine, Carla. *No time to say goodbye: Surviving the suicide of a loved one.* Main Street Books, 2011.

Furnes, Bodil, and Elin Dysvik. "A systematic writing program as a tool in the grief process: part 1." *Patient preference and adherence* 4 (2010): 425-431.

Harvard Health Publishing, Harvard Medical School. "Grief can hurt — in more ways than one." Febuary 19, 2019. https://www.health.harvard.edu/mind-and-mood/grief-can-hurt-in-more-ways-than-one.

Hewett, John H. *After suicide.* Vol. 4. Westminster John Knox Press, 1980.

Jackson, Jeffrey. *SOS: A handbook for survivors of suicide.* Washington, DC: American Association of Suicidology, 2003.

James, John W., and Russell Friedman. *The grief recovery handbook, 20th anniversary expanded edition: The action program for moving beyond death, divorce, and other losses including health, career, and faith.* Harper Collins, 2009.

Kübler-Ross, Elisabeth, and David Kessler. *On grief and grieving: Finding the meaning of grief through the five stages of loss.* Simon and Schuster, 2005.

Lewis, Clive Staples. *Grief observed.* Zondervan, 2001.

Lukas, Christopher, and Henry M. Seiden. *Silent grief: Living in the wake of suicide.* Jason Aronson Incorporated, 1997.

Merriam-Webster. Accessed May 26, 2022. https://www.merriam-webster.com/dictionary/bereaved#:~:text=noun,is%20bereaved%20comfort%20the%20bereaved

Online Etymology Dictionary. Accessed May 28, 2022. https://www.ety-monline.com/word/grief.

Salvatore, Tony. *Recovering from suicide loss: Self-help for individuals and families who have lost someone to suicide.* Morton, PA: Survivors of Suicide, Inc., 2008.

Salvatore, Tony. "Life after suicide. How emergency responders can help those left behind." *EMS magazine* 39, no. 2 (2010): 54-57.

Traylor, Elaine Schoka, BERT HAYSLIP, Patricia L. Kaminski, and Christina York. "Relationships between grief and family system characteristics: A cross lagged longitudinal analysis." *Death Studies* 27, no. 7 (2003): 575-601.

Scott, Elizabeth. "What is Spirituality?." Very Well Mind. November 27, 2020. https://www.verywellmind.com/how-spirituality-can-benefit-mental-and-physical-health-3144807.

Shneidman, Edwin S. *The suicidal mind.* Oxford University Press, USA, 1998.

Speaking Grief. "Grief Impacts our Brains." Accessed May 27, 2022. https://speakinggrief.org/get-better-at-grief/understanding-grief/cognitive-effects.

Speaking Grief. "Secondary Losses." Accessed June 3, 2022. https://speakinggrief.org/get-better-at-grief/understanding-grief/secondary-losses.

Sudak, Howard, Karen Maxim, and Maryellen Carpenter. "Suicide and stigma: a review of the literature and personal reflections." *Academic Psychiatry* 32, no. 2 (2008): 136-142.

Wolfelt, Alan D. *Understanding your grief: Ten essential touchstones for finding hope and healing your heart.* Companion Press, 2021.

Wolfelt, Alan. "Grieving vs. Mourning."TAPS. October 17, 2018. https://www.taps.org/articles/24-3/grieving-vs-mourning.

Worden, J. William. *Grief Counseling and Grief Therapy: A Handbook for the Mental Health Practitioner.* New York: Springer Publishing Company, 2018.

Wrobleski, Adina. *Suicide--why?: 85 Questions and Answers about Suicide.* Afterwords, 1989.

Acknowledgements

This journal would not be possible without the love and support of my family. My husband Rob has been by my side since day one, always loving and supporting me, even when I am not so easy to love. He has held me up, sat in silence with me, been by my side at support groups, attended many suicide prevention events and so much more. My two amazing children, RonnieMarie and Dante, who from the womb were involved in suicide prevention and awareness efforts. Thank you for your work and support not only helping your Mom, but other grieving individuals.

This book would not be what it is without my incredible editor and daughter, RonnieMarie.

Thank you to the many grieving individuals who have shared their story and journey with me. I have grown so much and benefited more than you will ever know by being part of your process. Without you I would not be doing what I do today.

Finally, I am grateful for my loving Father and God who has carried me through the valley of trouble into the Door of Hope.

And there I will give her her vineyards and make the Valley of Achor a door of hope. And there she shall answer as in the days of her youth, as at the time when she came out of the land of Egypt

Hosea 2:15

About the Author

Linda Falasco, LCSW, LICSW, is a licensed clinical social worker, therapist, consultant and lecturer. A graduate of Temple University with a Master's Degree in Social Work. She has received extensive post master's training in child develop-ment, bereavement, suicide loss and suicide pre-vention. She maintains a private clinical practice in Newtown Square, PA, where she works with individuals, families, and couples struggling with loss and grief, trauma, and mood and anxiety disorders.

Over the past 27 years she has developed various trainings and has been a sought after speaker for conferences on Suicide and Suicide Loss. After the tragic loss of her middle brother to suicide, she has poured herself into the field of suicide prevention and helping others with suicide loss as a labor of hope and love. She was the driving force in bringing a chapter of AFSP to Philadelphia and was one of the first board members. She has co-cordinated the first Survivors of Suicide Conference in Philadelphia and is the co-founder of the Delaware County Suicide Awareness and Prevention Task Force. She is the founder and coordinator for the Annual Candlelight Vigil Remembering Those Lost to Suicide. Find out more at lindafalascolcsw.com.